A Child's Garden of Grass

(The Official Handbook for Marijuana Users)

Jack S Margolis
and
Richard Clorfene

Illustrated by Jack S Margolis

BALLANTINE BOOKS • NEW YORK

ISBN 0-345-30496-9

This edition published by arrangement with
Price/Stern/Sloan Publishers, Inc.

Manufactured in the United States of America

First Ballantine Books Edition: September 1978
Fourth Printing: September 1981

First Canadian Printing: October 1978

DEDICATION

To the tortured soul of Harry J. Anslinger, former head of the Federal Bureau of Narcotics. If it weren't for him, we wouldn't have a book.

NOTE FROM THE AUTHORS

We have never smoked marijuana, and never will. But our friend, Ernie Lundquist, has. He told us all the stuff that's in this book.

Jack S Margolis
Richard Clorfene

Canter's Delicatessen
Hollywood, California

P.S. Ernie lives at 2120 North Highland Avenue, Apartment B, Los Angeles, California 90028. He keeps his stash in his shower curtain rod. Now that the book is finished, we don't need him anymore.

A NOTE ABOUT THE EPIGRAPHS

At the beginning of each chapter we have included a complete poem selected from Robert Louis Stevenson's collection of poetry entitled "A Child's Garden of Verses." Each poem seems to fit the material of the chapter it heads very well. Do you think that old Bob . . . oh, never mind.

INTRODUCTION

Hi! We're Dick and Jack.

TABLE OF CONTENTS AND
OUTLINE OF MATERIAL

PREFACE TO THE ORIGINAL EDITION

The controversy currently raging in this country concerning marijuana (should it be legalized, is it psychologically or physiologically harmful, does it lead to the use of hard narcotics) has been well covered in numerous books. If you would like to read in this area, we suggest, *The Marihuana Papers,* edited by David Soloman, (Bobbs-Merrill Company, Inc.); *Marijuana Myths and Realities,* edited by J. L. Simmons, Ph.D., (Brandon House); and *Pot, A Handbook of Marihuana,* by John Rosevear, (University Books).

Our personal viewpoint has been arrived at through a tremendous amount of research: We have read an enormous number of books, articles and essays on the subject; the first listed author has lectured or debated about it in front of numerous church, parent organizations and other special interest groups, appeared on national television shows devoted to the subject, and discussed it on a daily all-talk show which he hosted; and, finally, we know at least 200 people who use it on a relatively continuing basis.

Our viewpoint, without defending it here, is simply that marijuana is not harmful in any way either psychologically or physiologically, does not lead to the use of hard narcotics, and should be made legal, subject to the same or similar regulations which now apply to the use, distribution and sale of alcohol and tobacco.

PREFACE TO THE CLIFF HOUSE EDITION

For years my publishers have urged me to up-date this book, but I've always felt that was like asking Leonardo da Vinci if he would mind putting a little more color in Mona Lisa's cheeks.

When you've got a masterpiece, I always say, don't mess around with it. That makes for some pretty boring conversation, but it's what I always say.

But now, a little more than four years later, and after 750,000 copies have been sold and paid for (at four different prices, in four different covers, and by three different publishers), I figured that for the fifth cover and the fourth publisher, maybe it did deserve a little added pizzazz.

In going through the book, I found that the price you pay for grass, the penalties if you get caught, and the section on smoking accessories and paraphernalia are the only things which really require additional comment.

Prices

In Chapter V, in the section on "Buying Grass," we refer to kilos. Grass no longer seems to be sold in kilos (2.2 pounds) but in "bricks" or "pounds," which contain from 14 to 16 ounces.

Those who sell grass in smaller quantities break the brick into anywhere from 16 to 20 portions, and then sell each portion (still called a "lid") from $10 to $25.

A pound sells for from $120 all the way up to $800. The $800 a pound grass is purported to be "Colombian tops-only," but anybody who pays more than

$350 for a pound of any kind of grass is simply buying status.

And that's silly, because you can always buy a pound for $200 and *tell* everybody you paid $800.

By the way, Colombian has now replaced Acapulco Gold, Panama Red and Michoacan as being the pot smoker's *ultima thule*. Of course, if you want to be really hip, you've got to buy pre-Colombian grass.

Anyway, when reading this part of the book, change "kilos" to "pounds" and you'll be about right in terms of the prices.

The Penalties

The penalties for smoking and possession have diminished somewhat in some states, and a state by state breakdown (along with the Federal penalties) is included in a new Appendix provided at the end of the book.

This and other information comes to us through the courtesy of Keith Stroup of NORML (National Organization for the Reform of Marijuana Laws). If you're interested in even the slightest way in decriminalizing or legalizing grass, then you should support NORML. They are dedicated, hard working and very much underpaid people who feel deeply for the tens of thousands of people who are now sitting out harsh terms in prison for marijuana offenses.

[For the law-and-order conservatives out there, you might be appalled to learn that it costs approximately $1500 to arrest and process a person accused of marijuana possession. Since almost 400,000 people were arrested in 1976 on that charge, it cost us over *half a billion dollars* in that year alone to pursue our present course.]

Membership in NORML costs only $15.00 a year, and you get a regular newsletter and all sorts of extra stuff. And you get to help to bring a little sanity to a world going rapidly bananas.

Smoking Paraphernalia

In the section on "Smoking Grass" in Chapter VI, we mention a three-hole smoking device which we called a "Steamboat" because it sort of looked like one, with the top hole resembling a smoke stack when grass was burning in it.

But now they're called "carburetors," because they mix air with the grass. Personally I'm disappointed. Steamboat is more imaginative, and is easier to say. You can waste whole minutes trying to say "pass me the carburetor."

Also, in the last four years, more advancement has been made in the development of grass paraphernalia than in any other scientific discipline, with the possible exception of space technology and the naming of new pills.

There are now beautiful and practical things being manufactured for grass that help you grow it, cure it, weigh it, clean it, stash it, hold it, light it, smoke it and put it out.

There are literally hundreds of different new tools, and hundreds of different styles of each tool. The world's largest manufacturer and distributor of grass accessories puts out a beautiful color catalogue with over a thousand different items. The company is Berney-Karp, (Glass Head), 2850 E. 44th St., Los Angeles, California 90058, but they sell wholesale only.

A Note About The History Of This Book

This book was first published by Contact Books of Los Angeles in October, 1969, after being turned down for a solid year by fifteen New York publishers. Their reasons were always based on the fact that the book took an advocacy position on grass, and grass was not just against the law, it was *really* against the law. In fact, in many states, like Texas and Georgia, you could kill a person and get a lighter sentence than if you sold just one joint to somebody.

Now, of course, the penalties are much lighter. In some states killing a person and selling somebody a joint gets you about the same sentence—depending, of course, on who you kill and how good the grass is —although in some states, like Oregon, the penalties are about the same as that given for a traffic ticket.

In 1970, Ron Jacobs urged me to write an album based on the book, which I did with the late Jere Alan "Wacco" Brian. Jacobs used twenty people, tons of electronic equipment and four months to come up with what has been considered (never mind by whom) to be one of the best produced albums ever. It's on Elektra (EKS 75012), and your local record store will order it for you. Be sure to listen to it on a good stereo set, after taking the euphoriant of your choice.

And that's it. When you finish the book, please share it with a friend.

> Jack S Margolis
> Hollywood, California
> May, 1974

The History of Grass

The world is so full of a number of things,
I'm sure we should all be as happy as kings.

Grass was first discovered in Twin Falls, Idaho in 1907 by a small Polish immigrant by the name of Wayne Krulka. The discovery occurred in early May, while Wayne was working late in his study one evening, trying to find a shorter route to India.

CHAPTER II

The Effects of Grass

I should like to rise and go
Where the golden apples grow;—
Where below another sky
Parrot islands anchored lie,
And, watched by cockatoos and goats,
Lonely Crusoes building boats;—
Where in sunshine reaching out
Eastern cities, miles about,
Are with mosque and minaret
Among sandy gardens set,
And the rich goods from near and far
Hang for sale in the bazaar;—
Where the Great Wall round China goes,
And on one side the desert blows,
And with bell and voice and drum,
Cities on the other hum;—
Where are forests, hot as fire,
Wide as England, tall as a spire,
Full of apes and cocoa-nuts
And the negro hunters' huts;—
Where the knotty crocodile
Lies and blinks in the Nile,
And the red flamingo flies
Hunting fish before his eyes;—
Where in jungles, near and far,
Man-devouring tigers are
Lying close and giving ear
Lest the hunt be drawing near,
On a corner-by be seen
Swinging in a palanquin;—
Where among the desert sands

Some deserted city stands,
All its children, sweep and prince,
Grown to manhood ages since,
Not a foot in street or house,
Not a stir of child or mouse,
And when kindly falls the night,
In all the town no spark of light.
There I'll come when I'm a man
With a camel caravan'
Light a fire in the gloom
Of some dusty dining room;
See the pictures on the walls,
Heroes, fights and festivals;
And in a corner find the toys
Of the old Egyptian boys.

THE BEGINNER

Because of the controversy regarding the subject of grass, very little has been discussed about the effects derived from its use, and what has been discussed has given the wrong impression. This is probably because the effects achieved are very subjective and very allusive. Using grass is somewhat like making love or going to St. Louis (to use two extremes), you really have to have done it in order to know what it's about. We will, however, try to illuminate as many areas as possible to the best of our ability which, you will quickly find, is extraordinary.

We assume our audience to be both those who have never used grass and those who have tried it, perhaps many times, but still want to know more about it.* We will thus try to cover all phases of grass from the very first time one tries it to the time when one learns to use it as a tool not only for euphoria, entertainment

---

* We also notice in our audience a bus load of small elderly women from Schenectady, New York. You may stay with us, if you like, but please don't speak out or rustle papers.

and joy, but also as a tool for learning and understanding the world around him, and the world within him, too, if you want to be cute.

The first time a person tries to get stoned he may not feel any effect whatsoever. Many people, even after smoking themselves blind, and on good grass, feel no effect for the first two or three times—and there are some who report no effects even after ten times. It is, of course, possible that out of three point four billion people in the world, there must be some whose system just will not react with grass. For those we recommend needlepoint, weightlifting or any of the other traditional methods of reaching nirvana. We believe that except for these two or three weirdos, everybody can feel the effects of grass if they simply get over their fear of losing control. Your mind, if sufficiently motivated, can keep you from feeling the effects of grass just like the minds of fanatic mystics can keep their feet from feeling the hot coals they like to walk on so much.

Aside from the problem of fear of losing control (which is relatively rare), there are other barriers. Getting stoned, strangely enough, is a learning experience somewhat like swimming. While some people take to the water right away, others struggle for a long time.* Fortunately, there are known reasons why some people can't seem to get high, and these barriers can be easily overcome.

The first barrier to overcome is the person's belief that smoking pot gives one a "kick." It does not. There is no jolt or sudden overflowing all encompassing feeling. There is no instant or major change. The effects come on slowly and smoothly. Many neophytes thus don't think that they're stoned simply because they're waiting for the non-existent kick.

The second barrier is that there is no way to know how you are "supposed" to feel. Unlike being drunk,

---

* Read our book, *A Child's Garden of Water,* wherein we compare swimming with getting stoned.

the effects which are achieved when stoned on grass are subtle and nearly limitless in variety, and may differ each time you get high.

We once asked our friend Ernie Lundquist (see Note From The Authors, page 4) what the difference in feeling was between being stoned on grass and being drunk on alcohol. His answer was probably quite profound and very revealing, but unfortunately we can't remember what it was. At the time he was stoned and we were drunk.

You can usually predict approximately how you're going to act and feel when you get drunk: loss of control, dizziness, tight numbness, inarticulation, and nausea. With grass there are no predictions other than that you will depart slightly from reality. Right away, a whole bunch of people are screaming, "What is reality? Getting stoned is reality!" To these people we have one piece of advice: Don't confuse us.

The areas of reality which are departed from are physical, psychological and spiritual, but since the spiritual world is highly individualistic and purely personal, and is also inhabited by scary things like ghosts, goblins, and gods, we'll discuss only the first two.*

If you are having difficulties getting stoned, you might be afraid to let yourself go. It's easy to control a grass high, and the fear of knowing yourself may be overwhelming the high. As a great man once said . . . now what was it that he said? Oh, well, it doesn't matter. Anyway, the best way to learn what it is to be stoned is to have a teacher or a guide to help you.‡ Unlike LSD guides, a grass guide really doesn't have to be smart, sensitive, or extremely experienced. Any friend will do, the only requirement being that he or

---

* Once, when Ernie was stoned, he saw his Uncle Dave, who was over six feet tall and weighed 300 pounds. And what is worse, Dave was living in Butte, Montana at the time.
‡ The term "guide" was stolen from LSD Manuals, which in turn stole it from the Boy Scout's Handbook.

she has used grass before and can articulate his feelings.

A good guide will help a neophyte to feel the grass fully on his first trip. This is because one of the effects of grass is to cause a person to become suggestible, and when the guide tells the neophyte what he should be feeling, it will most often be felt. Usually, at this point, the neophyte says, "I do feel that, but only because you told me to. The grass isn't doing it." When the guide answers that the heightened degree of suggestibility has been brought about by the grass, the neophyte will have a tendency to disbelieve him. For some reason many people prefer to believe that grass will have no effect on them, and this is another barrier which keeps the neophyte from getting high the first time.

The guide, besides commenting on what is going on physically with the neophyte, should also give him something to eat, and let him listen to music, all the while pointing out various phenomena. The guide, too, should be stoned because his empathic abilities will then be increased, and because he won't have to relate the feelings he had from memory.

Another common occurrence on the first, second, or even third trip, is that the neophyte may be obviously stoned and do or say some strange and amazing things. Someone will ask him, just as a gag, "Are you stoned?" "No," he'll insist, and the insistence that he is not stoned will persist until the grass wears off, at which point you remind him of what he did or said. When he remembers, an embarrassed look will creep over his face and he'll admit that maybe he was stoned. However, the next time out, he'll once more reject the possibility of any effect taking place. Don't worry about him. He won't worry about you.

Then there's the neophyte who, throughout the entire time he is stoned, keeps asking, "Well, am I stoned?" Be kind to this person, he is reaching out for love.

If you're worried about where to find a guide, don't.

It has been a sustaining rule of mankind that one will always appear. It's been in all the folklore, mythology and theology for over 2000 years. One day a tall stranger will come into your village and talk you into trying some, and you will. Grass smokers are the world's greatest proselytizers, and should be out hustling for "The Watchtower." They are relentless. If you have a friend whom you know uses grass, and this friend knows you don't, and he has never offered to turn you on, look for a new friend. This one doesn't really like you.

PHYSICAL EFFECTS

The first mild sensations may be felt instantly after smoking half a joint, or an hour after having eaten some. Usually you creep slowly into a stoned condition, inch by inch sliding upward, but if you've eaten it, it may come on you suddenly, and strike you full force in the middle of a word. If the latter happens, it may sound like this: "So while I was shopping in the market I saw this fantastically beautiful chick, and I wanted to meet her. I was just about to use the 'drop the jar of mustard on her foot' ploy, when she . . . uh . . . what? What were we talking about?" And if the people you're talking to are stoned, they won't remember either.

Getting stoned suddenly and with full force most often is typical of having eaten rather than having smoked the grass. The reason is probably that an hour after you've eaten the grass, you've partially forgotten about it, and are therefore unconscious of the early barely perceptible signposts of being stoned.

The first sensation you will feel will be physical; a new tingling of some sort, a band of light pressure around your temples or in your shoulders or back. You become aware of your knees or your instep, or your head seems heavy and filled with chopped brown paper, or it might feel empty and floating farther above your shoulders than it's supposed to. You might also become aware of your anus or genitalia.*

Your body might become warm or cold, but rarely enough to cause any real discomfort. And you will relax. This relaxation almost instantly melts into a quiet contemplative euphoria, and a soft muting of everything from the corners in your room to the texture of your chair. Suddenly you're through the looking glass. It's your bedroom or living room all right, and everything is exactly the same, but everything is exactly different than it ever was before you were stoned. And suddenly you don't care about your arthritis, or that you have to appear in court the next day because of a speeding ticket, or that you've got a mid-term paper due in two days, or that you've only got one ear. Because suddenly you've discovered that the grain in the wood in the paneling on the door looks like the ripples of water when a rock is lobbed into a calm pond. And the photograph with the black border is suddenly given an interpretation because of the black border which now signifies something. And there's a feeling going through your entire body that is sensual and exciting and you start to dig it. And everything is great and you just want to sit there and enjoy it.

You'll also discover that grass is an analgesic, and will reduce pain considerably. As a matter of fact, many women use it for dysmenorrhea or menorrhagia when they're out of Pamprin or Midol. So if you have an upset stomach, or suffer from pains of neuritis or neuralgia, smoke grass. If pains persist, smoke more grass.

PSYCHOLOGICAL EFFECTS

Sometimes the early psychological changes coincide with the early physical changes experienced while

---

* If this happens, concentrate on it. Get to know it. Make it your friend.

stoned, but the famous mind-expansion (defined by us as pushed out of shape) comes after the first physical sensations.

One of the important things to remember when stoned is that grass distorts and heightens your awareness of both the outside world and your own psyche. This heightening and distortion sometimes work together, often resulting in confusion because you're not sure of whether you're seeing something more clearly than before or just differently.

Profound Revelations

Here comes another one of those conclusions that will send a lot of people into fits of pique: There is no such thing as a profound revelation while stoned! At the time of the thought, you may think that when you reveal it the universe will shake, but if you can recall it later when you're straight, you'll laugh at its insignificance.

The definitive story of false profundity concerns a well-known writer who, one evening while stoned (on something other than grass—but the principle is the same) was struck by a revelation of universal truth. He was overwhelmed by its significance and managed to bring himself back to reality long enough to scramble to his writing desk and frantically scribble his new-found wisdom on a scratch pad. The next morning our hero awoke, remembered that he had had some kind of vision and leaped out of bed to read what he had written. He picked up the piece of paper and read: "There's a funny smell in the room."

For those of you who still disagree with us, ask yourself this: In all the thousands of hours you have spent stoned out of your mind, have you ever once conceived of or invented something, or combined things in a new way, that had permanent substance and meaning? Oh, you've probably found a new way to interpret Dylan's "115th Dream," or you may have discovered a hitherto invisible burst capillary just beneath the skin on an inner thigh of a friend, or you may have drawn a groovy flower—but really profound, never. Ginsburg is right. Grass is fun.*

The fact that Samuel Taylor Coleridge saw a vision of the fragmented "Kubla Khan" while under the influence of laudanum (a liquid opiate), was shaken from the vision by a knock on the door, and, when he returned to write, the vision was there no more, weakens our argument not at all. Coleridge was a phenomenally gifted poet when he wasn't stoned on opiates; "Kubla Khan" is one of his least important poems; laudanum isn't grass; and who knocked on the door?

Here are two "profound" revelations revealed to our friend Ernie while he was stoned: "Survival of the species is everybody's business," and "No matter how much you dislike pickles, it is, after all, the only thing that you can do with cucumbers." At the time, Ernie was quite excited with these revelations and made an attempt to call the President to tell him about them.

What may cause this magnification of the importance of certain things is that your mind seems to be racing along, and, sometimes, operating on a number of levels at once. Coupled with the fact that you often have a tendency to forget everything almost as it happens, certain thoughts take on secondary and even tertiary meanings, and the whole thing can become very confusing.

Let's listen in on a quiet scene in the house down the street. Andy and Virginia are very stoned, and spending the evening listening to their collection of old records and giggling a lot. Right now "The Syncopated Clock" is on the gramaphone. Shhh, Virginia is going to speak:

VIRGINIA: Are you hungry?

ANDY: No. (Long reflective pause.) Wait a minute. Did you mean am I hungry for food, or am I

---

* That's Allen Ginsburg. Ralph Ginzburg is also right.

hungry in the abstract, like hungry for knowledge or adventure?

VIRGINIA: What were we talking about?

ANDY: You asked if I were hungry.

VIRGINIA: Did I?

ANDY: Yes.

VIRGINIA: Well, are you?

ANDY: Am I what?

Time and Space

Your awareness of time and space also becomes confused. Things seem to take an unearthly long time, although sometimes, much less often, things which should take a long time, seem to have zipped by in an instant. Zipping slips by in an instant. Unzipping seems to take forever.

Our friend Ernie says he'll never forget his first experience at a rock music concert while stoned. The group playing was the Doors and the first number was an eleven minute song called, "When The Music's Over." Two minutes into the song, Ernie leaned over to his girl friend and asked, "How many songs have they played?" "This is the first one," she replied. "Oh," Ernie said, but two minutes later he leaned over again and asked, "How many now?" "How many what?" she asked. "How many songs have they played now?" "One. Just one," she said. "Come on!" Ernie said, in disbelief. "No, really." "Oh," Ernie said, unsatisfied. Two minutes later, Ernie leaned the other way and asked the stranger next to him, "Say, how many songs have they played?" The stranger answered, "Uh, wow, uh, you got a cigarette?" A minute later the stranger leaned over behind Ernie and began talking to Ernie's girl friend, and before the song was over the two of them split.

Space alteration is totally unpredictable. Sometimes the room looks longer or shorter. The ceiling is three floors above you or an inch from your head. Maybe there will be no space alteration in your room whatever, but get up and walk down a flight of stairs and that flight of stairs becomes infinite.

It should be obvious that things which require good judgment of time and space should be scrupulously avoided when stoned. Things to especially avoid are cooking an egg, driving a car, and tight-rope walking.

Time disorientation can sometimes cause you needless concern. Who hasn't experienced having his girl friend say that she is going to the kitchen for some Tab, and then not see her again for two days? After concern that she has accidentally locked herself in the refrigerator, or been spirited away by Caryl Chessman, you run into the kitchen and yell, "What's the matter?" only to realize that she's been gone a minute and a quarter.

Hung-upedness

There is also the experience, known clinically as "Hung-upedness," which strikes everyone, regardless of race, creed, color, political posture or place of national origin of the grass. Small tasks or insignificant things take on a tremendous importance and interest. Often you find yourself doing some little thing over and over, like scratching, or picking lint off of your dog, or staring at a tiny spot on the wall. Sometimes when you run into the kitchen to find out what happened to your friend (see above if you've forgotten about your friend), you'll find her closely examining the tiny splashes that the dripping water makes in the sink. She probably has forgotten all about the Tab that she wanted so badly—which is just as well. Dietetic soft drinks are for the weak in spirit anyway.

Time distortion and hung-upedness act together quite often, and you find yourself doing something inane for a long time and thoroughly enjoying it, even though every now and then you think you've been doing it forever.

When you do do something dumb, such as to watch "The Price Is Right," or "The Flying Nun" on TV, another symptom is revealed. After staring like idiots at the show for eighteen minutes, someone will ask, "Why are we watching this stupid nonsense?" You will all turn and smile and nod at the one who asked the question, then resume your watching, as will he who spoke, until the show has concluded. Why? Because a basic truth about being stoned is that everything is good. Nothing is bad. Some things are phenomenally good, but nothing is phenomenally bad (except getting arrested—but even *that's* a learning experience).

Funnyness

This is one of the most pleasant and exciting psychological changes which occurs. There's a little spot in your mind which tells you when you think something is funny and grass expands that little spot until that little spot takes over and everything is funny. Everything. Your friend's teeth are a riot. A simple "Hello" brings on storms of laughter. And something which is genuinely funny, like hearing a good joke or watching the Marx Brothers can turn you into a convulsive maniac, writhing in agony and pleading for help. Going out in public in this mood can be a risky act because of the laughing problem, as you find yourself laughing at people who are not stoned and fail to see what is so amusing. Sometimes they hit you.

Passivity and Inertia

Passivity is another of the signposts of the stoned condition. Everyone is more passive when stoned than when straight. This does not mean that everyone is passive when stoned in the pure sense of passive. Hell's Angels get stoned a lot and they're not passive. They're mean and nasty. But imagine just how mean and nasty they'd be without grass. They'd probably get rid of their little bikes and buy tanks and steam rollers to run you over with.

The story which capsulizes this passivity isn't very

funny, but it's valid. If you haven't heard it before we claim to have made it up. Three men come to a walled city at midnight. A sign on the bolted door in the wall to the city reads, "This Door Will Remain Locked Until 9 a.m. Tomorrow Morning." Just by coincidence, the three men happen to be an alcoholic, an acid head, and a user of grass. (Yeah, you guessed it. It's one of those rotten three part jokes.) After reading the sign, the alcoholic says, "Let's break down the door." The acid head says, "Let's just float through the keyhole." And the grass user says, "Let's sit down and wait for tomorrow morning."

See, we told you it wasn't funny, but it's true. And true is more important than funny. Of course, when you've got a funny truth, then you've got something.

One of the reasons for this passive feeling is the law of inertia, which results from the fact that whatever you're doing at that moment is too good to leave.

If you're lying quietly in bed listening to music and enjoying your ecstatic joy, someone invariably says, "Let's go out." They want to take a walk, or eat, or whatever. This becomes the last thing in the world you want to do. All you want is to lie there and listen to the music. But finally you get up, put on your clothes, and start to go—and now you're filled with excitement about your adventure. Nobody, no matter what, could ever get you back into that bed. Well, maybe not *nobody*.

The rule is that your body, if in motion, will tend to stay in motion unless acted upon by an outside force; and if it is at rest, it will tend to stay at rest, unless acted on by an outside force. Say, that's pretty good.

This whole thing could be very dangerous to your budget if you happen to wander into a store while stoned. Because you will like everything, you'll want to start buying things. And once you start, it's hard to stop. So avoid stores of any kind, especially supermarkets. They are the deadliest because they combine these qualities with that of the importance of food.

Enter a supermarket and you will ram things into your shopping cart that you never noticed before, like Pez candy or banana flavored Maypo. You can't possibly pass by the smoked oyster section—those pleading eyes and those little tails wagging with joy at seeing you. And at the check stand you'll probably make an offer on the shopping cart because it's fun to get pushed around in. And you're going to be very confused the next day as to what to do with twelve pounds of mangoes.

Our friend Ernie once let this buying tendency get the better of him. One day when we were in his posh Highland Avenue apartment, we noticed a hundred and twenty assorted little glass pigs sitting on four walnut bookshelves hanging on the wall. You know, the kind you buy along with a pole lamp, just after you graduate college. We didn't think Ernie was the kind of guy who'd collect little glass pigs, so we asked him about them. "I don't collect them," he said, sounding slightly angry, "I bought them all at once last week when I was stoned." "What do you do with them?" we asked in unison. "Nothing," he answered. "Don't you ever look at them?" "Yeah," he said, "sometimes. But only if I'm stoned."

Meditation

Meditation is a method of discovering hidden aspects of the world or of one's self, or of transcending reality in order to reach a higher spiritual state. One method of accomplishing it is to concentrate for long periods of time either on a specific theme or subject, or a meaningless word (mantra).

Meditation is a practice relatively common to certain Eastern religions, but it is (at least until recently) rather foreign to most people in the Western world. This is probably due to the differences in the style of living which exist in the two worlds.

The people of the East are used to a slower paced, less confused and more serene type of existence. Their temperament is more suited to the act of meditation (sitting quietly for hours, even days, contemplating certain aspects of the inner or outer world) than is ours.

Westerners are more oriented to articulating their problems or questions; that is, they talk about them (or, sometimes, write about them). If a Westerner has a problem of alienation or confusion, he is apt to see an analyst. The Easterner is more apt to meditate about it.

Most Westerners find that meditation is impossible, and dismiss it as being irrelevant or meaningless. This is a shame because meditation is a rather pleasant and, occasionally, profitable exercise.

Transcendental Meditation, explained by Maharishi Mahesh Yogi and popularized by the Beatles, is supposedly a drugless way of becoming "in tune with the cosmos," or of reaching nirvana, satori, the clear light, or whatever you want to call the state of pure and absolute bliss. Since Transcendental Meditation provides a faster method of reaching your meditative goals than other forms of meditation, it is more in tune with the rush and excitement of the Western world, and we recommend it.

Many people who have tried to meditate and failed (using this method and others), have succeeded when they were stoned. For some reason, grass considerably increases the ability to concentrate on the mantra, and to transcend reality.

Although most of the Eastern religions (the Maharishi's included) claim that you can reach the transcendent or metaphysical state without external stimulation, many Westerners have found that it is much easier with the aid of grass. After having learned how the whole thing works, most people continue meditating but without the grass. For those in a hurry to reach nirvana, we suggest that you attempt meditation (at least the first few times) while stoned.

The following is a bastard form of Transcendental Meditation which has worked for us:

First, get a mantra, a magical word that is meaningless in and of itself. Supposedly the word should come from the Maharishi or one of his teachers, and should be a word which is very personal and used exclusively by you. Being of a pragmatic nature, we fail to see why you can't make up your own magical word. Most mantras which we have heard of (and we gained this secret information through the usual methods of kidnapping and torture) have four syllables, with the first syllable stressed.

We will give you a mantra, but remember, this is a personal mantra, and you're not to tell anyone what it is. It'll be a secret among ourselves. Shhh. Your mantra is "oon-yellimon," with the first syllable stressed.

Now, sit on the floor or on your bed, with your feet crossed and your hands in your lap. Sit up straight. Take a deep breath and relax. Let your mind wander for a while as it usually does. When you find a space in your thinking which seems sort of quiet, start saying the mantra—but not out loud and don't vocalize or move your lips. Stress the first syllable hard, and keep saying it over and over. If you have to scratch or move, do so, but no matter what happens in your mind, keep saying the mantra. And concentrate on it as long as you can.

After a while, stop saying the mantra, and relax your mind. Let whatever happens happen. You may hallucinate, or you may reach a poignant peak of euphoria, or, and this is more likely, nothing may happen. If nothing does happen, keep trying. It may take a few days of work, but it's worth it.

After you've gotten where you want to with meditation while stoned, try it without grass. Grass should be used only as a learning tool.*

* Ernie used to meditate quite a bit while stoned, but has recently given it up. He said that he finally saw God, and God told him to stop meditating.

The Holy Three

Now we get to the most important things which grass alters, and, through alteration, enhances. These things are three, the holy three, and they are eating food, listening to music, and making love.*

Eating Food

Eating becomes a joy unbounded. All food tastes great. If you open a box or bag of stuff like Abba Zabba bars or dried figs you'll start eating and eating until someone happens along and pulls the bag or box out of your hand, at which point you might dash to the refrigerator and start eating lettuce or leftover pieces of fried squash.

Chinese food is ambrosia. A milkshake comes direct from Aphrodite's breasts. Chopped liver quells your rampant anti-semitism. All food is wonderful. So wonderful, in fact, that even though your stomach is full up, you'll still want more.

If you get stoned a lot, you'll probably end up with a weight problem. Therefore the most practical food is that which takes a long time to eat. One couple we know gets stoned almost every night and watches television. They've hit upon what they think is the perfect food: Root beer and pistachio nuts. The root beer is for their thirst, of course, and the pistachio nuts for their flavor and, more importantly, for the fact that it's hard to open them. Thus a small amount lasts them a long time. They've also discovered that about 10% of the pistachio nuts in any bag are impossible to open. They put these aside and only eat them when they feel that they've gained too much weight.

If you're going to be in a very comfortable and stationary situation, you don't want to keep getting up

* If you're clever, you might even think of a way to combine all three.

and running to the kitchen, so be sure that you surround yourself with various foods before settling down. Spread little bowls around the room filled with pistachio nuts, pinto nuts, individually wrapped chocolate drops, and sunflower seeds.

We personally suggest lumpfish caviar (it's cheap), sour cream and teeny crackers of some sort. Besides tasting great, it takes a long time to get the caviar jar open, and almost the entire night to put sour cream and caviar on each one of those teeny crackers.*

If you're going to have company over, keep in mind that everyone will have a dry throat and a nearly unquenchable hunger. If you don't have plenty of munchies and suckies around the house when the gang drops in, the gang will leave and so will you.

If you do leave, you'll head for the nearest good restaurant. Look for a well lighted place so you can appreciate what the food looks like, and you can watch the other people coming and going.

We recommend the following types of restaurants:

Italian	Jewish
Turkish	Russian
Chinese	French
Mexican	American

We suggest that you avoid the following restaurants:

Latvian	Canadian
Norwegian	Tierra del Fuegan
Andorran	Howard Johnson's
Paraguayan	

By the way, has anyone else noticed how difficult it is to find a good Icelandic restaurant these days?

---

* Warning! Don't *look* at the caviar and sour cream because when stoned the texture appears all green and awful.

Music

Listening to music while stoned is a whole new world. Most heads consider its importance second only to sex in the realm of tripdom. And grass will change your musical habits, generally for the better, stoned or not stoned. If you hate classical music, get stoned and listen, even to something very sophisticated. The sounds will take on new meanings and you will hear structures, instrumentation and passions which you never had the capacity to hear before. And often you'll get an insight into what the composer was trying to do, even though you've had no experience with classical music before.

We're convinced that the Hi-Fi and stereo boom is to a great extent due to the fact that so many people are now getting stoned, because music, when stoned, becomes another world: intricate, three dimensional, visual, and completely understandable both intellectually and emotionally.

Many people who had previously rejected sophisticated music now love it due to exposure while stoned. The word "appreciate" means both to like and to understand, and you seldom really like something which you don't understand. If you haven't had a background in classical music—if you weren't brought up on it—you may not like it simply because you don't understand it. Normally it takes a lot of exposure to serious music before you can understand it, but grass, for some reason, gets you into it right away. Grass makes it understandable and exciting the first time you listen to it.

If we still haven't convinced you, try this little test. Get stoned and play the last part of Tschaikovsky's 1812 Overture; the part just before the end where the music goes down the scale. We guarantee that it will feel, *physically,* like a run down a ski slope or an orgasm, depending on where your head is.

Electronic music, often disturbing and silly sounding

while straight, becomes truly funny when stoned, although you might find intricate rhythms and sound patterns that make you hear this music as music for the first time.

Why does rock music appeal to someone who's stoned? Because the good stuff is full, rich, exciting music. People who would have been composing "serious" music a hundred years ago are composing rock music today.* What about those nonheads who are musically oriented? Why do they snobbishly reject all rock music as trash? Perhaps because grass is the catalyst. Maybe you need to be stoned to assimilate the same themes and counterpoints and harmonies which are used in classical music, but which, in rock, is coupled with a primitive driving beat. And the lyrics, rich in imagery, metaphysical conceits, symbolism and inside allusions to grass argot, may be too obscure for the straight person. Rock music is written by and for heads. It's a rather well-known fact that almost all rock groups are heads, and most of the writing and composing is done while they're stoned. Although most heads buy a lot of rock music, it's not created strictly for the sole purpose of amusing stoned people. But, as Ernie once said, "Those who take care of us, we take care of right back."

After all we've said about music, perhaps now you understand why musicians were the first major group of people to start using grass.

For those who have recently started smoking grass and are not into music, we recommend you listen to the following:

Classical music
Folk and Acid Rock
Electronic music
Jazz

* In fact, they even *look* the same.

We suggest that you *not* listen to:

Myron Florin music
Dick Contino music
Florian Zabach music (unless these three are all
    playing together)
Elevator music
Polkas

Sex

A feeling which occurs quite often and rather strongly when stoned is a thing called sex. It is a good idea not to get stoned unless you have a girl with you —unless you already are a girl. If you already are a girl, Hi there. Our names are Dick and Jack. Would you like to come over to our house and see our new orange shower curtain?

The strange thing about sensuousness while stoned is that sometimes it's confused with the feeling of sleepiness. Both feelings extend throughout your entire body, and are very similar. This is true. But it takes almost only a moment's thought to redirect a sleepy feeling into that of a sensuous feeling. It is, however, almost impossible to redirect it back again. Once your body experiences sensuality, it doesn't want to leave it. Don't fight this, because your body knows more about these things than you do. Follow its lead.

Because the effects of grass on sex is so enormous and important, we've devoted an entire chapter to it. If, for some strange reason, you're interested in this subject, see Chapter III, Grass as an Aphrodisiac.

Unpleasant Effects

Marijuana is a euphoric plant with mild sedative powers. It creates extremely happy moments for its users by allowing them to get deeper into things and thus get more out of them. Besides causing him to be able to laugh easily and readily, grass also causes the user to be pleasantly pensive or meditative, romantically orientated, sensually sensitized, open, accepting, and buoyant; only occasionally does it cause unpleasant experiences. The problem rarely occurs, but since it raises several vital questions in every neophyte's mind, we will deal with it fully. In fact, we will give it more emphasis than it really deserves, which may tend to scare off some people. This merely points out our elevated sense of sadism.

Grass changes reality. It creates the feeling that you are somewhere other than you really are. Thus, the experience is often referred to as "taking a trip." If the experience is particularly intense and places you in a specific point of unreality for a sustained period of time (even a minute), it's called "tripping out." If the specific point of unreality is very unpleasant or lasts a long time, it's called "being on a bad trip." If it's only mildly annoying, or merely lasts a moment, it's called "being on a bum trip," or, more commonly, "a bummer." A bad trip and a bummer are qualitatively and quantitatively different things.

These terms are now part of the marijuana argot but they are also perfect to describe a part of the human condition that is all too common. People go on bad trips or bummers whether they're on grass, alcohol, pills, or nothing, and they probably always will. A bad trip is almost always characterized by depression or anxiety, and we doubt that there is a person in the world who has not experienced these feelings, at least mildly, at some time in their lives. Let's consider these feelings in terms of a person who is not stoned—who is straight.

The worst possible manifestations of depression are hysterical crying, overwhelming self-pity, or suicidal wishes (but since Camus tells us that suicide is the only valid philosophical question, perhaps it's good for all of us to consider it at some time, especially those of you who don't like this book). In the worst moments of an anxiety attack, you may become paralyzed with fear, super-angry, or just very jumpy.

What causes these bad trips? Well, Gestalt psychologists believe that we perceive the world in terms of patterns, and bad trips usually seem to occur right after the person has suddenly recognized an unfortunate pattern in his life—a pattern which he seems to be locked into and doomed to repeat forever.

One of the most common patterns of recognition has to do with love affairs, or the difficulty in finding a mate (both the herd instinct and the desire for pair-bonding are very strong in all humans). A typical example is that of the single woman of twenty-five. She suddenly realizes that she has dated different men for maybe as much as ten years. Some of them have been meaningful relations and some have been only casual, but all of them are now over. She feels that she is doomed to repeat the same old nonsense: meeting men, dating, becoming involved, becoming bored (or being rejected) and breaking up. Over and over, she feels, she has done this, and over and over she will continue to do it.

She may now find herself in the throes of a bad trip. If she uses the recognition of the pattern to attack herself, believing that her own inadequacies have created the pattern, and that her life is meaningless and superficial, she will become very depressed. Conversely, if she recognizes the pattern but cannot pinpoint the reasons for it, she may project the whole of her existence as being doomed to repeat the pattern endlessly, like the characters in Sarte's "No Exit," and find herself in an advanced state of anxiety.

Of course, a recognition of almost any other unpleasant pattern will also cause these same feelings of depression or anxiety, but for the vast majority of people, all of these patterns are easily understandable and of an unprofound nature. A few other patterns which seem to be recognized with a certain frequency are: being trapped in a seemingly pointless career, an unhappy marriage, the inability to communicate honestly and openly, or nearly any aspect of the world which one wishes could be removed or altered. There are other reasons why a person may go into a bad trip, of course, but pattern recognition seems to account for the vast bulk of them.

If you've had these experiences, then you might have them to a deeper degree when stoned; and if you haven't had them before, you well might when stoned. The reason is that although you've thought of these things before and have been able to accept them or shrug them off, the influence of the grass gives them a distorted sense of importance and terribleness. It's rare to have them when stoned, but we feel that you should be aware that they might occur, so that you can be prepared for them. Again we might be scaring you needlessly, but our occasional desire to achieve integrity demands that we be honest. The odds against you having a very unpleasant trip are high, but they are something to consider. As our friend Ernie's grandfather once told him, "Just because horses occasionally poo-poo on the street is no reason to stop using horses."*

But you can get out of these rare bad trips very easily with the help of a friend—not a doctor or a policeman, but a friend. If you know how, you can do it yourself, although it's much easier with a friend —if he knows how. And where are you or your friend going to learn how? Many people have bad experiences which they could easily have avoided if only there was someone to tell them how. Unfortunately, because so many people believe that marijuana is bad (with no evidence to substantiate that belief), there is no way to reach those people who believe that marijuana is good, and who use it, but who occasionally have an unpleasant experience.

One of the terrible shames of this country is that no one will recognize that hundreds of thousands of peo-

---

* Unfortunately Ernie's grandfather was later trampled to death.

ple are using LSD, and millions, even tens of millions, of people are using marijuana. It is a fact of our existence, and passing more laws against it and using stricter methods of enforcement is not going to cut down on the use of marijuana and drugs. We live in a very sophisticated and complicated civilization, and there are many methods to circumvent the law, especially when it is a bad law, and when the desire to break it is great. Law enforcement and legislative officials are just as intelligent and resourceful as those who use marijuana, and every advance made on one side is met with an advance on the other—but marijuana users are more highly motivated to reach their aim than are those who are trying to suppress them.

Because of the ostrich-like laws governing the use of marijuana, when a bad trip gets out of hand, where can the person go? It's like the cliché movie scene of the gangster with the bullet in his leg. If he goes to a doctor or the hospital, he will be turned in to the police, so his buddy (played by Scott Brady) pulls out the bullet with a hammer and tweezers, and the gangster dies. The grass user is forced to play the role of the gangster in our society, and thus society, with one unthinking flourish of its pen, has created a whole new criminal class; one made up of millions of people.

Because for so long people were uptight about sex, there was little real sex education in schools, and almost none at home. People would claim to be very upset about the high rate of venereal disease and the high rate of illegitimate births, but would do nothing to stop the cause, namely lack of education. But luckily times are changing in this area, and, if you look closely they may be changing in the area of marijuana too. An ameliorative process seems to be under way, not because of press or pressure, but because police officials and legislators are turning on now too. There are signs that one day we will all be at peace with one another, but any delay is surely criminal.

How To Get Out Of A Bad Trip

It would be wonderful to have the advice and guidance of experts in the fields of sociology and psychology, but, until they are willing to come forward, we will have to do.

The first sign of depression or anxiety is often a feeling of nausea—as a matter of fact you may experience nausea and nothing else. The feelings which are recognizably depression or anxiety come later. If you begin to feel this nausea, simply begin thinking of something specific. Anything will do. Focus your mind on externals, or on a pleasant thought. The nausea will usually disappear.

As we've said before, it may be difficult to get yourself out of a bad trip, but relatively easy to help someone else. So, if you're going through a bad scene and you're alone, call up a friend and tell him what's wrong. Just talking about it will help tremendously.

All right, now you're with someone who seems to be having a difficult time. What do you do? (It doesn't matter if you're stoned too, by the way, because it's easy, usually, to bring yourself down when you want to.) You have two choices: Let him go through the bad trip in the hopes that although he'll be very uncomfortable, he may gain some insight into what is causing him to be frightened or depressed; or, get him out of it.

If he doesn't want to do the former, which is likely, then you're stuck with the responsibility of getting him to be happy again—but it's a relatively simple matter.

The first thing is to give him some tranquilizers. That is the advice of a friend of ours who is a psychologist, but it strikes us as a strange thing to give someone who is depressed, and anyway, pills scare us. This method, then, is optional, but we suggest avoiding it.

You remember from reading other parts of this

chapter that grass heightens and distorts one's awareness of both the outside and inside worlds, so you
know that what is bothering your friend, while perhaps valid, is being given more attention than it deserves, especially since he would rather be enjoying
himself. What is bothering your friend, then, is not as
terrible or as immediate as he believes.

You also remember that under the effects of grass
a person is highly suggestible. He will have a tendency
to believe what you tell him. So the first thing to do is
remind him that he smoked a lot of grass, and that
grass distorts reality—so whatever he's thinking is not
as bad or as important as he thinks it is. Then distract
him away from his thoughts. Tell him an exciting and
interesting bit of gossip or news. Show him an intricate picture or put on some pushy music. This
usually works.

Another thing you could do is change his environment. Turn on the lights if the room is dark, go
outside for a walk, or go into a different room. Be interested in him, don't ignore him, and keep up a
steady stream of babbling.

It may be that nothing is going to interest him other
than his particular chain of thought. The best you can
do then is to get him to talk about what is bothering
him. He will usually do this fairly readily, especially
if you convince him that by talking about it, he'll get
through the bad feelings it's causing him. All you
have to say is, "Look, you're not interested right now
in anything except what's bothering you. I can get you
out of it. Tell me what it is, and we'll talk about it.
Maybe it's the same hang-up I've got." Be calm and
reassuring and treat the problem in a logical manner.

Because he's in a highly suggestible state, if you've
done what we've suggested, and done it firmly and
with assurance, he'll rely on you with relief and be
guided out of his trouble. When he begins to talk
about his problem, his depression or anxiety will
slowly wane and he'll be happy again. The bad trip

usually lasts a short while anyway—and almost without exception will end by the time the high is over.

If you have tried all of the above, and used every resource that you know, and you still have failed (which is very unlikely), call a mutual friend whom you both respect and who has a natural knack for making people feel better.

Bad trips experienced because of marijuana are truly rare experiences. They may occur one time out of a thousand, or they may never occur at all, and there should be no concern about their severity. Both good and bad emotional states may seem to be strong and external, but they are transitory, lasting only until the stoned condition passes. Since this is almost never longer than three or four hours, and since a bad trip rarely lingers during the entire period, the anticipation of problems should be but a minor concern.

Grass shares almost nothing with the stronger hallucinogens, such as LSD, DMT, or mescaline when it comes to the risk of mental anguish. The entire concept of the Freak-out so often identified with LSD has little importance in marijuana use.

The Bummer

The bummer is an extremely mild form of unpleasantness of short duration. It occurs because of a sudden negative stimulus or as a result of "coming down," i.e., reverting back to a normal state.

A mild depression, or letdown, occurring after a good time is common for almost everybody. Most of us have felt mildly unhappy after coming back from a vacation and realizing we have to go back to work again (the Monday Morning Blues sort of thing). And probably a lot of people go through a post-coital depression from time to time, too. Coming down from a grass high is somewhat the same sort of thing.

Many people, after a three or four hour grass trip feel tired, mostly because they've been more active than usual, either physically or mentally. So a tired state and even a very mild form of depression, now that the wild feelings are over, occasionally may occur.

A bummer is the result of something that intrudes on your reverie causing you to either feel an unpleasant emotion, or to come down. While you're stoned, you're usually sensually stimulated, or keenly involved in a thought or an activity, and any interruption becomes a major intrusion, and its meaning may be exaggerated or distorted.

For example, if you are sitting quietly talking with friends and someone tastelessly decides that it would be puckish to hit you in the nose with a spitball, you could interpret the act as one of severe hostility and go into a bummer. You would then stare at the spitballer with such a look of contempt and pity that he too would soon be into a bummer. Then you would feel guilty for throwing him into a bummer and be into still another bummer. Then he hands you a slice of orange jelly candy and everything is fine again.

Perhaps you are at home with friends and you're all stoned and laughing, and the phone rings and it's your boss. You don't want him to know you're stoned, and if you don't control yourself while talking to him, you are certain you will giggle at everything he says or ramble on and on about meaningless things (trip out). If you do trip out, you're sure that he'll think you're rude, drunk, crazy, or, worst of all, stoned on grass, so you have to be calm and precise and it brings you down and bugs the hell out of you. That's another bummer.

One of the most common of the mildly unpleasant states which may be produced by grass is that of being paranoid. The feeling produced is not that of paranoia, which strictly refers to the rare cases of fixed and highly systematized delusions, but of a paranoid state, a state similar to paranoia symptomized by anxiety due to the irrational and unfounded fear that you are being persecuted.

But feeling "persecuted" when you are stoned is a fully justified and valid feeling in the vast majority of cases because what you are doing is against the law and there are real people who are really trying to arrest you. The feeling is indeed a bummer, but a protective one.

There is also, however, the times when a person is sitting safely at home with friends and begins to think that they are laughing at him, or talking about him silently using gestures. There is nothing to be concerned with if you experience this type of paranoid state. Because things are distorted, it is to be expected that you may not quite understand what is going on. If the paranoid state becomes too uncomfortable, simply mention it to the others. Ask them politely to stop laughing at you. They will instantly deny that they are laughing at you, and then begin to feel paranoid themselves because they think you're picking on them.

You'll have no problem whatsoever with paranoid states if you remember that it is not an uncommon state while stoned, it is due to confusion, and it passes quickly. But as our friend Ernie once said, "Beware, even paranoids can have real enemies."

Almost anything which starts unpleasant thoughts going through your mind, like witnessing an accident or hearing bad news, is a bummer, but bummers are easily shaken and are not very bad to begin with. The only real concern you should have with bummers is to be careful not to send those around you on one.

CHAPTER III

Grass as an Aphrodisiac

When I was down beside the sea
A wooden spade they gave to me
To dig the sandy shore.

My holes were empty like a cup
In every hole the sea came up
Till it could come no more.

IN GENERAL

Ever since the dawn of history man has been agonizingly pursuing the answers to two questions: "What is the meaning and purpose of life?" and, "Where can I get a good aphrodisiac?"

Aphrodisiac has been defined as "any of various forms of stimulation used chiefly to arouse sexual excitement." They have been classified into two groups: 1) the internal (foods, drugs, love potions), and 2) the psychophysiological (stimuli to one or more of the five senses, which in turn spur sexual desire).

The first group has received the most attention (probably because it would seem to be the easiest to use) in spite of the fact that, with one or two possible exceptions, there really is no such thing. Many people believe that certain foods or food combinations such as oysters and gin, or pepper, produce as aphrodisiac-like effect, but no scientific study has shown there to be sexual arousing qualities in foods of any sort, and it is thus generally concluded that food cannot produce sexual desire biochemically (i.e., by reacting internally with your body).*

Those who believe that certain foods are aphrodisiacs will admit, if pressed, that the reason for their belief is that these foods contain an abundance of vitamin E, sometimes known as the Love Vitamin. But whether vitamin E has any real aphrodisiac qualities is highly suspect. This belief may simply be the result of a neat job by the public relations firm who handles pharmaceutical houses engaged in the business of making Vitamin E tablets. (The same public relations firm probably sold restaurants on the idea of using parsley as garnish, on behalf of the International Parsley Cartel.) The habitual popper of Vitamin E's will admit, however, that he (always a he) uses them not for true aphrodisiac effects, but because he believes that the vitamin increases virility (although why anyone would want to take a pill that causes hairy forearms is beyond us).

There is also a genus of liquid intoxicants universally believed to be true aphrodisiacs, which includes Absinthe, Mescal, and Damiana. (While in Marrakesh, Ernie tried some Absinthe. Within three minutes of finishing his first glass of the notorious brew, he found an uncontrollable desire to change his name to Brian Donlevy and join the French Foreign Legion.) But forget Absinthe, forget Mescal and the rest of that stuff. There is no scientific proof that they work as an aphrodisiac, they do real and serious damage to your brain and liver, and they're almost impossible to get hold of anyway.

The most universally famous aphrodisiac of the first group is the notorious "Spanish fly," and, according to a strict interpretation of the definition, it would have to be considered as one of the real and valid aphrodisiacs.

Spanish fly is the common name for *Lytta vesicatoria,* which is a blister beetle (a Coleoptera within

---

* Recently, however, there has been some talk about Jell-O.

the Meloidae family—but you probably already knew that). This beetle is dried and powdered (at which point it is called "cantharides") and is used to raise blisters.* Cantharides acts as an irritant to the genito-urinary tract, and thus produces a painful kind of sexual desire. Along with cantharides, cocaine and certain other substances will (especially when applied directly to the genital areas) produce an itching or burning sensation which is translated by the mind into a craving for sexual release. One of the main problems with this kind of substance is that the craving it produces is often incapable of being satisfied for long periods, and thus it can result in severe mental anguish, or real pain.

When mature sophisticated people talk about an aphrodisiac, we think that they are talking about something which will increase the desire for sexual activity in a beautiful and controllable way. As the first group of aphrodisiacs contain only substances which are either mythical, or dangerous and painful, our only hope lies in the second group.

The second group of aphrodisiacs, the psychophys-iological, are almost infinite in number (although they are not specific things, like a drug, or the love potions which John Collier and others have written about). Almost anything which you perceive (see, hear, taste, touch, or smell) which pleases you, can, under the correct circumstances, arouse you sexually. As a mat-ter of fact, for a normal person, this goes on many times during the day. But usually, because we're hung up on other things, or we're just hung up, we submerge the feeling.

Surely you can recall the momentary excited feel-ing you've had when you've smelled a whiff of nos-talgic perfume, or when you've seen two butterflies spiralling over a flower, or when you've gotten up early on a bright warm Sunday. All of these kinds of things, these beautiful things, have aroused you sexually, al-

---

* A practice which seems to be dying out, especially on the West Coast.

though you may have misread the feeling because sex seemed inappropriate as a response in terms of the stimulus.

Even something as prosaic as food can produce a sexual response, although, as we've said above, food per se is not truly an aphrodisiac. But there is no question about the effect which a well-prepared meal of subtly seasoned foods can have upon the human organism. As the usually sexless Encyclopedia Britannica so enthusiastically puts it, "The combination of various sensuous reactions—the visual satisfaction of the sight of appetizing food, the olfactory stimulation of their pleasing smells, and the tactile gratification afforded the oral mechanism by rich, savoury dishes —tend to bring on a state of general euphoria conducive to sexual expression." In other words, if a wife complains that her husband is not making love to her enough, it's probably because she's a rotten cook.

The above quote contains the key to discovering a more valid and useful definition of aphrodisiac than the one we used at the beginning of this chapter. An aphrodisiac is, "The combination of various sensuous reactions . . . (which) tend to bring on a state of general *euphoria* conducive to sexual expression." And, as you remember, the chief effect of marijuana is to cause you to feel euphoric.

Liquor, of course, has been the traditional euphoria producing tool of the seducer, and the line, "Drink up, honey," has echoed down the hallways of history, reflecting man's desperate hope that if he can't get laid based on his own charm and intelligence, then he might if he can get a woman so drunk that she won't know what she's doing. And, often, he succeeds, but the result is sexual intercourse between two people with at least one of them not being sure what is happening up to, during, and after the experience. This is hardly a way to produce a beautiful and meaningful experience, but it is an apt way to engage in some pretty dreary and desperate fooling around. Seducing a drunken woman is as satisfying and stimulating as winning a philosophical argument with a dead gold-fish. And besides, she might throw up.

There is little question that both grass and liquor break down the defenses and destroy the inhibitions—those artificial restraints based on a sometimes unconscious conditioning resulting from the fiats and preachments of disoriented moral leaders who believe that sex is the weapon of the devil. But they work in different ways and for different reasons.

Liquor adversely affects your abilities to perceive and conceive. When you're drunk, your ability to see, hear, taste, feel, or smell, or to think clearly and imaginatively, are temporarily impaired, if not almost completely destroyed. And the drunken woman more easily engages in intercourse not because she desires it spiritually, emotionally, or intellectually, or because she likes the man she's with and wants to share something beautiful with him; but because of some primeval urging basic to all organisms, built into her DNA to ensure the survival of the species.

Grass, on the other hand, heightens your enjoyment of your perceptions and conceptions tremendously. (You were wondering when we'd get back into the subject of grass, weren't you?) Therefore, all things considered, grass is the world's best and safest aphrodisiac, whether you use it for base reasons such as effecting a seduction, or for ennobling reasons, such as wanting to provide your loved one with the most possible pleasure for the longest possible time.

Grass causes the feeling of just being alive, of existing, to become a joyous surge of passion, because everything around you is so smooth and shimmering and glorious. The use of grass also often produces synesthesia (which is the effect of perceiving a stimulus with a sense other than the one being stimulated); thus feelings which are usually understood with only a part of you (such as visual pleasures) begin to be subjectively perceptible with all of your being.

The music in the room or the murmurings of your friend are not just an audial delight, but a physical sensation. The smell of your friend's hair, or the warm soothing touch of their body, or the curve of their cheekbone, all these separate sensations swirl and mix together into a whole, an avatar—a divinity incarnate. And the sensual delight of your own body and the glorious splendor of the setting all fuse together and you and your friend and the whole world become one charisma of jubilation, for minute after minute after minute until a millenium has passed and the time has lost all claim to meaning. And the multitude and inter-mixtures of responses that you experience preparatory to and during the sex act seem to recur again and again (like the infinite number of images produced when you stand between two mirrors) and they begin to reproduce themselves and intertwine with one an-other, growing and building until you experience reve-lations of feeling so poignant that you can examine each pinpoint of pleasure, and so overpowering that the entirety of it thrusts you into a maelstrom of pure ecstatic energy. Or, as Samuel Pepys so often wrote in his diary, "And so to bed."

There are four areas in which this heightening of the sexual response is clearly manifest: Foreplay, control, orgasm, and creativity.

Foreplay

Foreplay is classically the woman's problem. Mar-riage manuals, usually authored by sexually frustrated psychologists who sublimate by writing about dirty things, always tell us that women have to be slowly and gently brought to the level of sexual desire, whereas men, like some sex crazed animal, become filled with a frenzied lust immediately upon seeing a flash of thigh on a windy downtown street. Well, to some extent and in many cases, they're right. Except for couples who have been married for many years (where the situation is often reversed), the man is usually sexually ready immediately while the woman is not. It becomes necessary, then, for the man (or his assistant) to arouse the woman through foreplay so that she will be where he is when they begin intercourse.

Here again grass comes to the rescue like some melodramatic bow-tied hero, and with a money back guarantee. Being stoned on grass will increase a man's interest in foreplay. It is simply another extension of Hung-upedness. If one can get hung-up for ten minutes by splashing drops of water from a faucet, imagine what one can do when confronted with the sight of a pair of heaving breasts, or the smooth curving feel of full hips and firm thighs. Every part of a woman's body contains a vast variety of temperature, texture and resiliency, and each time they are touched by a different part of the man, it is as if they were newly discovered. Grass awakens the Lewis and Clark in every man.

And foreplay works both ways. Men don't need it to become sexually aroused as do women, but they want it, and grass will infuse the woman with a desire to explore and discover; and wonder of wonders, she'll find that this turns her on too.

Control

The problem of control—or the avoidance of premature ejaculation—is a major contributing factor in the disasters which often occur in the boudoir. This is not as rare an occurrence as one might think, and, in desperation, men have tried many methods to avoid it. One of the classic methods men use is to think of something repulsive, such as garbage, while they're making love; but it seems tragic that someone has to go through life knowing that every time they make love they're going to think of garbage. You'd think he'd eventually give up making love.

There are other methods, such as concentrating on reciting the alphabet backwards (silently, we trust), masturbating an hour or so prior to the act, or spreading some kind of anesthetizing balm, such as Nupercainal with Benzocaine, on their penis.* While these methods occasionally accomplish their mission, they always lessen the man's passion, separate him mentally from his mate, and remove most of the beauty and purity of the event.

For the man who has this kind of problem, grass is the answer (we hope you're beginning to realize just how wonderful this book really is). One would think that because grass heightens everything, it would make control even more difficult, but the reverse is true. Perhaps the way it works is that the grass makes every moment of the event so overwhelmingly pleasant that one unconsciously wants to remain in the pre-orgasmic state as long as possible, and rather than the act being a means to an end (the orgasm) it becomes an end in itself—and the orgasm becomes something like a fringe benefit.

The Orgasm

The problem of achieving an orgasm has peopled psychiatrist's couches all over the land with women of every race, creed, color and standing in her community. It has been estimated (by people who seem to have an awful lot of free time) that as many as 50% of American women fail to have orgasms. (We wonder if much of this isn't the fault of the researchers.) There are also many women who can achieve orgasm, but not through intercourse.

Well, we hate to keep harping on this, but when you have a panacea, you have a panacea: Grass will help in every way. The use of grass will enable most women to achieve an orgasm easier and faster, will cause the orgasm to be more intense and of a longer duration, and, in some cases, will enable her to have what

---

* Ernie claims that anything which contains 1/10th of 1% benzoate of soda, such as peanut butter, cottage cheese, or horseradish, also works. Ernie has very few girl friends right now.

Esquire magazine has called a status symbol, the multiple orgasm. Perhaps it works because the effects of the grass allow the woman to get away from the hangups of her mind and into the swirling sensations of her body.

It's possible, of course, that with grass the man does not really have more control, it just *seems* as if he lasts longer. And it's possible that the woman doesn't really have longer or deeper or more orgasms, it just *seems* that way. Well, in the final analysis, it doesn't make any difference, does it?

We're not copping out—we believe that the above effects are real and not simply illusionary, but it's difficult to prove it without a laboratory such as the one which Masters and Johnson have.* And because people act differently at different times, and differ from one another, we cannot assert that the above effects will happen to every person every time. But it's axiomatic that grass improves your ability and increases your pleasure in all areas of sexual activity, and that it's a learning tool that will allow you to get more out of your sex life even when, later, you're not under its influence.

Sexual Creativity

By creativity we mean experimentation and innovations of a sexual nature. That is, all those things you might do which go beyond plain old everyday Protestant intercourse. We don't, however, want to get into the question of perversion in this book,‡ because it's so subjective. The feelings about it range all the way from Cotton Mather, who would feel shame when he took off his hat, to Lenny Bruce, who once said, "The only act I've ever done which I would con-

---

* Our friend Ernie tried to set up such a laboratory once, but he failed because his equipment was substandard.
‡ But see our next book, "A Child's Garden of Some Simply Awful Things."

sider perverted was jacking-off my dog." We don't even know if we would agree with Lenny Bruce— we haven't seen his dog.

You're going to do only that which you enjoy and nothing more, and you're not going to harm anyone, so it doesn't matter what your neighbors say or what some cobwebby government agency thinks is "right." So we aren't going to talk about it very much. Live and be well. But grass will help you to find new pleasures, new meanings, and new ways to express your love for your partner. It will open you up to new ideas, and expand your repertoire. Who knows what may happen. The man who has previously found sexual expression only through that lone position certified by the Talmud may find himself embracing the Kama Sutra. And the old Mineral-Oil-Rub-Down-On-A-Plastic-Tarp trick may simply become an old stand-by laugh getter. And conversations like this may occur:

HE: I really dig it when you do that.
SHE: Why didn't you tell me? I really dig *doing* it.
HE: Why didn't you ask me?
SHE: Spiro, do you love me?
HE: Just keep doing that.

Environment may become important, and you may find yourself fixing up your bedroom or living room (or kitchen, if you're *that* kind of freak) so that it provides you with an atmosphere that is a true extension of your sexual fantasies.*

The only suggestion we'd like to make to add pleasure to your environment is that you get yourself a black light and put it in your bedroom. The light softens everything and gives it an other-worldly surrealistic effect, and it makes everyone look beautiful.

* Ernie once moved the backseat of a 1938 Dodge with a wax dummy of Edward Kienholz on it into his bedroom.

It makes the skin appear to have a deep perfect tan (and if you're a Negro, please try to remember that black is beautiful).

HOW TO USE GRASS AS AN APHRODISIAC

Based on all that we've said above, we're sure that you're convinced that grass is an aphrodisiac; but if you believe that whenever you turn on you will automatically become sexually aroused, you're mistaken.

Grass removes sexual inhibitions, not by numbing the mind, as does liquor, or by directly affecting your body, as does cantharides, but by increasing the pleasant feelings of your body and by enhancing the beauty and serenity of your environment—but your environment often contains aspects which are easily as enjoyable and interesting as the sexual experience. Therefore you may be totally immersed in the pleasures of drawing little figures with a rapidograph, or dancing, or talking, or listening to music, or walking in your garden—and your mind may not be on sex at all. And of course this is great. Sex isn't everything. It may be a huge part of it, but it isn't everything.

However, you may have inferred from the title of this section that we were going to tell you how to exploit grass for your own selfish sexual ends. Well, although we would rather see you walking in your garden or listening to music, we'll help you a little bit.

If you and a friend are stoned, and you find that you are in a sensuous mood and wish to culminate the feeling in a fruitful manner but your friend is in another mood, you have two tools at your disposal. One is that your friend is pre-disposed to feeling sensual anyway, and the other is that he or she is in a highly suggestible state.

You could, of course, use the direct approach, and simply say, "Let's make love" (or any suitable variation). By suggesting that you make love, you've planted the thought in the other person's head. That thought will grow and blossom, unless, unfortunately, it's killed by the weeds of disgust at your lack of charm. Use the direct approach only if you have a time problem, such as, for example, having to catch a train in ten minutes.

If you really want to seduce a friend or your spouse, and they're stoned, simply do the things you normally do. If you usually strike out, then you'll still lose, but far less often; and if you're usually successful, you'll be more successful.

One feeling relatively common while stoned, especially among people who are new at it, is being tired. But the feeling of being tired and the feeling of sensuousness is very similar. This may sound weird, but it's true. The next time someone says that they're tired, explain to them that they're misinterpreting the feeling, and that they're really feeling sensuous, and they will! One of the wonderful things about grass is that once you learn to understand it, you can manipulate your own mind to produce almost any feeling or emotion that you want. And also, to a large extent, you can influence other people's minds, too.

By this we mean only that if you're feeling depressed, you can feel happy. If you're feeling cold, you can feel warm; and if you're feeling tired, or anything else, you can feel sexually aroused; and you can effect these changes in others, too.

If you really want us to give you some pointers about seduction, we will—but only in private consultation, and only if you're a lady. The men can stay clumsy and ineffectual for all we care. That leaves more for us.

CHAPTER IV

Games

Bring the comb and play upon it!
  Marching, here we come!
Willie cocks his highland bonnet,
  Johnnie beats the drum.

Mary Jane commands the party,
  Peter leads the rear;
Feet in time, alert and hearty,
  Each a Grenadier!

All in the most martial manner
  Marching double-quick;
While the napkin like a banner
  Waves upon the stick!

Here's enough of fame and pillage,
  Great commander Jane!
Now that we've been round the village,
  Let's go home again.

IN GENERAL

So far we've been concerned primarily with the physical and emotional aspects of being stoned. It's time now to discuss the mental aspects. Virtually every mental activity one engages in when stoned may be lumped into the broad category of games, partly because everything seems like a game when stoned, and partly because the competition and excitement of playing games become heightened and validly reflects our entire life struggle.

It's not entirely clear why games are so singularly fascinating to heads, and we wish that Marshall McLuhan would quit fooling around and start applying his fine mind to something worthwhile like this question. In McLuhanesque terms, games become a temporary medium when one is stoned. Being stoned itself is a potent medium according to McLuhan's definition of medium, and it's approaching a serious rivalry with television as the control medium which is shaping and altering our society. Certainly grass controls fewer people than does television, but to those it does serve as a medium its influence is even greater than that of television, as inconceivable as that might sound to non-users of grass.

As a matter of fact, TV itself is influenced tremendously by grass. The montages, kaleidoscopes, music, quick cutting, brilliant flashes of color, language, etc., are all a result of the new worlds which the grass and drug user has discovered. And conversely, TV educates the non-smoker that there's a more beautiful world possible inside his own mind, and as soon as the non-smoker begins to realize that the new uses of the visual and audial medium he is exposed to on TV are the result of grass (inter alia), then he'll have a greater tendency to eventually turn on. TV and grass are scratching each other's back.

The thing which grass and games have in common is that they are both escapes. Many people believe that the word "escape" has an ominous sound. People who have to escape are weak people according to those involved in the Puritan Ethic. Work is good, they preach, and those who escape from it are bad.

But today, in the United States, there is not really enough work for everyone, and the only thing which can keep society peaceful and functioning is for people to find escapes.

But what does the word "escape" really mean? What is an escape and what isn't? Is a person who spends Saturday night reading a book escaping from the real world, from people and society? Is the person who goes to a party on a Saturday night escaping from trying to expand his knowledge by reading or studying? Is a man who takes his work home from the office trying to escape from his wife? Is a man who sits at home at night with his wife watching television or arguing trying to escape from the work he should be doing for the office? And isn't going to work everyday, spending eight hours adding up somebody's account books, or defending someone in court who has been accused of building his house seven inches over someone else's property, really escaping from sitting by a stream with a fishing pole and thinking about himself and the world?

In other words, everything you do is an escape! An escape from what? From death. But as you're a long time dead, and only a short time alive, it seems valid to assume that you should make every moment as rich and meaningful and vital and multi-dimensional for yourself and those around you as you possibly can.

Thus we believe that games, which add another dimension to your life, and grass, which heightens all feelings, mixed together create an exciting and enriching escape.

There are two basic game phyla: physical games and intellectual games. A few games, of course, fall into both categories such as Stick Quiz. This is a simple game played with a leader and one or more other people. The leader asks a question of one of the other players. (A typical question might be, "How many kinds of fish can you name?") If the person doesn't know the answer,* then the leader gets to hit him with a stick. We don't like this game so much.

* Seven.

OUTDOOR GAMES

When it comes to the physical games, there are but two things to remember: keep them simple, and bear in mind the problems with space and time which you'll have. Mumbley Peg or Russian Roulette, or for that matter all games involving knives or guns are out for obvious reasons.

Baseball is out just on general principles. Football, La Crosse, hockey, polo, tennis or handball are also out, and you may want to avoid all other game-like sports which pit you against another person, since the mere physical competition may, when you're stoned, cause you to feel that your opponent is demonstrating his previously hidden hatred for you simply because he wants to beat you. If you must engage in this kind of game, go after the more delicate forms, like ping pong, badminton, or croquet. (Playing croquet while stoned, by the way, is an extremely beautiful trip. Sometimes you think that you're a member of English aristocracy, and sometimes you think you're God.)

If you want to feel completely safe, play only those games in which the competition is yourself, as in bowling, golf, or weight lifting. Of these we recommend golf most strongly. Bowling can be problematic. Until you've been glared at while stoned by a bowling alley cocktail waitress in her black satin slacks with the yellow stripes running down the side, simply because you order ginger ale instead of beer, you don't know what hostility means. And weight lifting is all right, but the stoned weight lifter has a tendency to lose track of his repetitions past four. And he might suddenly hear a clear voice in his head say, "What in hell am I doing all this stupid work for?" and revert back to a happy and non-sweaty 97 pound weakling.

But golf is a wonderful thing when stoned. The very things which make this game so aggravating to non-heads make it charming when stoned. A vicious slice that sends you across three fairways and into the woods is a major trip. While looking for your ball you may find a cute little chipmunk or a mother robin feeding a fat juicy grub to her young. While teeing your ball, you may find that unless the tee is perpendicular to the ground, the ball will fall off (a profound revelation?). It could take you fifteen or sixteen tries until the ball stays on the tee, and while normally this might be upsetting, when stoned it becomes hilarious to you and to the rest of your foursome, if they too are stoned. Warning: Make sure that they *are* stoned. Otherwise as your buddy is about to negotiate a difficult uphill lie with a six iron and you shout, "Hey, Fred, look at this great flower!" he is almost certain to become very angry.

INDOOR GAMES

Outdoor games are all right, but they lack the intellectual challenge, the imagery and the superworldliness of indoor games.

The intellectual level of the games which will be most fun for you when stoned depend on how stoned you are. If you're very very stoned, you might have trouble playing "Find Your Foot" or "Peek-a-Boo." But if you can maintain a normal level of awareness, a myriad of games are available to you which present new excitement and challenges which you never would have guessed existed.

Children's Games

Since a stoned adult often recaptures the beauty of a child's enthusiasm, wonder, and innocence, children's games are worth investigating, particularly those which demand some degree of physical dexterity and concentration.

Pick-up-Sticks is a good example. This silly little game takes on new dimensions when played while stoned, and you'll approach its unique problems with meticulous forethought and planning, often thinking five or six sticks ahead.

But the most interesting children's games, and the ones which sustain interest for the longest periods of time, are those which allow you to create something. Fingerpainting, Tinker Toys and building blocks are excellent examples. Combine four or five sets of building blocks during a party, sit everyone on the floor, and begin to construct something, each person placing a block on the structure in turn. No matter how you fight it, your effort always turns out to be a Gothic Cathedral and all participants sit back proudly, and bask in their own sunlight.

Board Games

When it comes to board games, you can derive intellectual pleasure from anything from Rich Uncle to Monopoly to Go. But they do more than provide intellectual stimulation; they provide a combination of all the emotions possible.

Let's look at Monopoly for a moment. You're spending a quiet evening at home with your wife and another couple. You've all gotten stoned, and someone suggests that you play Monopoly. You bring the Monopoly set down from the closet shelf. It's dusty because four years ago you swore you'd never subject yourself to the extreme boredom one faces when playing Monopoly. Then you blow the dust off the box and open it, and it's a new surge of excitement. It's nostalgia mixed with challenge. You think for a moment of the kid next door who used to win all the time, and who told you filthy and impossible things about girls. You weep openly upon seeing the mustachioed face of the man on the Chance cards, and you revisit the childhood hours you spent on Marvin Gardens and Illinois Avenue. You look with contempt at Baltic Avenue and with wonder at Boardwalk. And then the game begins.

You screen the world out, replacing it with a world

Arnold Rothstein knew and loved. The gold $500.00 bills are more real than anything the U.S. Treasury could ever print.

You pick the toy cannon for your move-piece because you always had the toy cannon as a kid because it was lucky. And you look at the three friends around the table, and they aren't friends any longer, but antagonists. They are Gould, Fish, and Doheny and they want to rule. And you break into a maniacal laugh, because you know you will win.

And when the dice are tossed and you land on a railroad it's a unique experience. If Monopoly had been invented last year you would land on American Airlines, and how dull that would be. But the mispronounced Reading Railroad! Drama, passion, a page from a romantic era. And you realize how fragile life is, being buffeted about on the hot breath of the old hag Lady Luck. You gnash your teeth at "Luxury Tax" and take a deep breath of relief at "Free Parking."

The victories and defeats of Monopoly don't relate to the outside world, but to the person who plays the game when stoned, they are more important and more delicious than the real ones.

Monopoly is a part of almost everyone's childhood, and thus as a game it has more significance than others, but there is one game which is unique. This game is so great that if this book does nothing more for you than turn you on to it, your investment will have been a wise and fruitful one. The game is called Go, and has been a Japanese national pastime for over 3,000 years.

This book is not really the proper place to go into all the aspects of Go, but let us say here that it appeals not only to the rational and abstract levels of the mind, but has real audial, visual, and tactile beauty, and is also a truly spiritual game. And although it's capable of being played, at least on a superficial level, by women and children, it makes Chess seem like a simplified form of tick-tack-toe.

One word of caution. Go (and other games) take on more meaning and are played with a greater depth of feeling if played while stoned, but your game will not be as good. The reason is that you have a tendency to get totally involved with a certain aspect of the game, and fail to see the total picture.

Puzzles

These classify as games, although they are almost always played alone. Therefore their appeal is different from other games. There is no competition, unless you put a stopwatch on yourself to see if you can unravel the mysteries of the puzzle faster than someone else. The variety of puzzles available is limitless, and collectors of antique puzzles number in the tens. Most of the puzzles that hold the greatest fascination for the beautiful people are the Oriental wooden pull-apart-and-put-back-together variety. These come assembled in the shape of a ball, a cube, or a barrel—although inside they are exactly the same puzzle. Only the outside has been shaped differently.*

The new mind-busting games such as "Hexed" and "Instant Insanity" are a progression of the old puzzles, and depending on how you view the uselessness of spending hours to master an intricate puzzle, you'll love or despise these games when stoned. Without question, you'll get involved, all hung up, and either not be able to put your puzzle down for hours, or get hopelessly frustrated in a minute and throw the whole thing out a window. Whichever way it goes, it pays to have a puzzle or two around that you have mastered, so when you go to someone's house someday who has the same puzzle, you can pretend to be a novice and dazzle the crowd with the dexterity with which you put the thing together. Life can suddenly be made to work for you if you employ this theory in everything you do.

* Why is this?

Psychic Games

When it comes to psychic phenomena, we're a couple of drags. It never ceases to amaze us that practically everyone we meet nowadays, whether it be a waitress in a short order cafe or a professor of Romance Languages, asks us what sign we were born under inside of the first ten minutes of the meeting. To avoid this nonsense, we simply tell people that we're ashamed of our signs; they're shabby rundown signs, and we don't tell them what our signs are until they start hitting us.

If you're hung up on any spiritual system from numerology to talking to your dead Uncle Steve, good luck to you. You're certain to open up to it even more when stoned.

Two spiritualistic diversions that have captivated hippies and weekend heads around the country are Ouija and Tarot Cards (but watch out for I Ching and the Enochian Tablets—they're real comers). Our friend Ernie Lundquist is a Ouija fanatic, as you may have guessed and he works his board religiously. But no matter how hard he tries, it keeps spelling "potato." *

Games of Thought and Talk

You'll find that you'll probably turn to the talking games when you're stoned at a party, because they're the easiest and most fun, and they need no gimmicky aids. Talking games range from the simplest and most unstructured, such as Trivia, to the very demanding, such as Botticelli. In between are Ghost, 20 Questions, Pass It On, and Two For Flinching.

The following is a collection of new game concepts which we developed specifically for grass parties.

---

* We would like to discuss Tarot Cards, too, but unfortunately we are forbidden to.

Imagery

The group pretends that they speak a language with millions of words in it. Because of the highly developed level of abstract thinking and sophistication, each word of this temporary society's language embodies a whole idea with an incredibly specific reference. One person makes up a word, and each tries to think what that word means. The sound of the word has no reference to the meaning (because that is another game entirely).

One person might say, for example, "grellsen." One of the other players, after thinking for a moment, of course, might say that a grellsen is "one who hunts the golden tiger with contempt and disdain." This person might also point out at this time that a "grellton" on the other hand, is "one who hunts the silver tiger upon a horse of dubious ancestry." At this point, the next player informs him that he is mistaken; a "grellsen" is the past tense of the verb "to grell," which means "to sit in a quiet corner of a dance hall and, while watching a fat couple dance the tango, untie the shoe of a man at the next table." He could also, at this point, state that "grellton" is simply the pluperfect tense of "to grell."

If anyone doesn't want to play this game, he has to roll the next joint or go out for more food.

By the way, you'll be surprised how quickly you'll tire of this game.

Make A Sentence

Each person in turn says a word, and as the words come, a funny, interesting, revealing, or dumb sentence is formed. A variation is for each person to make a sentence in turn, thus forming a whole story. But as you forget the word or sentence a few moments after it's said, this turns out to be a very stupid game.

New Trivia

You play this game just as you play old Trivia,
except that in New Trivia there is no reference to
movies, sports, radio shows, comic books, or the like.
Just old friends from childhood that the other people
can't possibly know. When one is guessed, it's an event.

Bridges

In case you've never heard of this game, in spite of
its growing popularity, one person names as many
bridges as he can. The main advantage of this game
is that it's over very quickly.

CHAPTER V

Acquiring Grass

Through all the pleasant meadow-side
   The grass grew shoulder-high,
Till the shining scythes went far and wide
   And cut it down to dry.

These green and sweetly smelling crops
   They led in wagons home;
And they piled them here in mountain tops
   For mountaineers to roam.

Here is Mount Clear, Mount Rusty-Nail,
   Mount Eagle and Mount High;—
The mice that in these mountains dwell,
   No happier are than I!

O what a joy to clamber there,
   O what a place for play,
With the sweet, the dim, the dusty air,
   The happy hills of hay!

IN GENERAL

Before you can do anything with grass, you, obviously, have to get some, and this is not always an easy thing to do. There are four basic methods of acquiring grass: buying, growing, receiving as a gift, and stealing.

BUYING GRASS

In buying grass, there are four things to remember: First, you don't want to get caught; second, you don't want to get bad grass; third, you don't want to overpay; and we can't remember the fourth.

The first rule to remember in buying grass is "Know Your Connection." If you know and trust the person from whom you're buying the grass, you shouldn't have any difficulties. He won't be a cop or informer and, if the grass turns out to be a real burn (less than the correct quantity or bad quality), he'll probably make good.

The second rule to remember is, "Don't Trust Nobody." This applies even to people whom you know and trust. Undercover agents look and sound exactly like you do, and many informers are not actually agents; they're just people who have been put into the position of turning in other people because they themselves have been caught, and they've made a deal with the police.

Buying grass is usually relatively safe, because police usually bust people who sell it *to* them, rather than people who buy it *from* them. However you still may have cause to worry when buying it, as we've pointed out above, so here's how to allay some of your fears:

Cops usually work in pairs, so always buy it from one person.* If the seller shows up with a second person, forget it.

When arranging the transaction with a seller, you might say to yourself, "Why is he suggesting that I go to *his* place?" or, in the alternative, "Why is he suggesting that he come to *my* place?" Both thoughts seem to make you paranoid, and rightfully so.

Don't go to his place, because even though you're buying it, it could be a set-up where both of you are

_____
* Or three or more.

arrested and later the seller (who was working with the police) is let off. And don't let him come to your place, because it could still be a set-up, or your place could be watched later, and busted when there are a lot of people over.

You're probably saying, "Swell. What are we supposed to do, meet in Guam?" Well, don't be so snappish. The best thing is to have the seller follow you to the place of a friend, so that the seller doesn't know where it is ahead of time. After buying it, you duck out the back way and hide it or take it home, while your friend delays the seller from leaving by showing him dirty pictures.

If you're really paranoid, meet the seller at a large nudist camp. Then, while you're both naked (this avoids hidden microphones and tape recorders) take him to a secluded place. He sets the grass down by an oak tree, you give him the money and walk back with him. A friend of yours comes from the other side, puts the grass in a different package, and leaves. This process, you'll find, is fool-proof. Only eight people have been busted using this method.

Now that your worries about getting caught are out of the way, you still have to keep from getting burned (buying bad or cut grass, or getting less than the right amount).

If you know your connection, there should be no problem, but if you don't, then you should sample the grass first. Usually a seller will "puff" his wares— which means claiming that it's better than it is. Cases have held that puffing is legal, so if the grass turns out not to be as good as he said it was, you have no recourse in the courts. The smart thing is to bring some papers with you and sample it. (A seller of bad grass will usually say he is out of papers.)

As for the correct amount, an uncleaned kilo is about a normal shoebox full, packed very tightly. A lid, can, dime, or ounce will, when cleaned, almost fill a Spice Island spice jar. Uncleaned it's about another third.

Good grass means that the grass is mild, it gets you stoned fast, and you can get very stoned with it. Bad grass you have to smoke a lot of, and sometimes, no matter how much you smoke, you just can't get very high. And although good grass usually sells for more than bad grass, don't use the price as a measure of its goodness.

Price varies considerably depending on the time and place. The price of a kilo selling in Los Angeles is between $90.00 and $120.00. (Everybody talks about $70.00 kilos, but no one does anything about them.) In New York the price is anywhere between $175.00 and $250.00.

Acapulco Gold (and there is some confusion as to whether this is a separate species or simply a mixture containing only the top leaves) is rare and much more powerful than normal grass. Its price is sometimes as much as double the normal suggested retail selling price of regular grass. A lot of sellers claim to have Acapulco Gold; we recommend that you don't believe them for about a week.

In Los Angeles, an ounce of grass sells for $10.00. In San Francisco, it's about $12.00 to $15.00. In New York, it's about $20.00. Of course, if the market is flooded, the price might be less, or if the market is tight because of a lot of busts, the price will go up; but these conditions usually last a very short time. The rule of thumb is, "The closer to Mexico, the cheaper the grass."* But a smart shopper will always check the papers and buy during sales.

A kilo is equal to 2.2 pounds, or 35.2 ounces. If you buy a kilo for a hundred dollars, you can sell it an ounce at a time for $10.00. Which means you can make a profit of 25 ounces or $250.00 (although most keys contain two pounds even). Most "dealers" are simply people who are selling part of what they bought in order to get free grass.

---

* New York, however, is now beginning to get a lot of good inexpensive grass from the Middle East.

The best way to buy grass is to buy a kilo; you're cutting down the risk by cutting down the number of buys, and you're getting it cheaper (less than $3.00 a lid). If you do buy a kilo, be sure to sample it, and if the package is broken at one end—sample the other end.

The worst way to buy grass is by the joint, which sells for from 50¢ to $1.00 all over the country. There are about forty joints to an ounce, which means you would end up paying from $20.00 to $40.00 for one ounce.

This brings up one of the cute things that the police do. Every now and then you read in the paper about a big bust and there's a picture of some men burning "a million dollars worth of marijuana." Crap. For public relations purposes, and to justify their existence, the police inflate the worth enormously. Their method of figuring how much has been destroyed is based on fifty joints per lid at a dollar a joint. At fifty joints per lid and 35 lids per kilo, this amounts to $1750.00 per kilo, or 17½ times the retail price of a kilo.

On top of that you've got to figure that if a guy has hundreds of kilos, he must have bought them wholesale, which is at the most 10% of the retail price. (In Mexico, a kilo, when bought in quantity, sells for $10.00. In Viet Nam, according to a friend of ours who is a head and a war correspondent, and who spent two years over there, one kilo sells for $4.00.)

So if you divide the price which the police give by 175, you can figure out how much of his own money the seller actually lost. If the papers say the police confiscated a million dollars worth of grass, the dealer probably paid only about $6,000 for it.

A ton of grass bought in Mexico probably costs less than $10,000; therefore "a million dollars worth of marijuana" would be a hundred tons. You could fill up the Empire State Building, and you wouldn't have a hundred tons! (Maybe you would, we don't know. If you're going to try to find out, let us know and we'll help. We have as much intellectual curiosity as the next guy.)

All this talk about the cheapness of grass in Mexico should not get you excited. If you do buy grass in a foreign country, you should smoke it there. (If you must bring some of it back, be sure to hide it in your suitcase, or customs will find it and take it away from you.)

Although many people get across the border and through customs successfully, it's not worth the risk. The customs officers have the right to search you thoroughly and totally for no reason whatsoever. And their methods of search are getting more sophisticated all the time. (For example, the border guards at Tijuana now use dogs trained to sniff out grass—although the carbon monoxide fumes of the cars get the dogs sick rather quickly.*) And often the guy who sells it to you will notify the guards because he gets his grass back and/or a reward.

If you're travelling, you'll find that grass grows naturally in almost all parts of the world. The best grass, however, grows in Lebanon, but because they use almost all of it to make hashish it's difficult to buy it there.

GROWING GRASS

Growing grass is a long and scary process, and it's almost not worth the trouble. The only good thing about growing your own is that it's free. So if you don't care about growing grass, we won't mind if you skip this chapter. Just don't tell us.

Grass grows easily throughout most of the United States, especially in the central states, and Tennessee, Georgia, California, and Kentucky. As a matter of

* If you have to cross the Tijuana border with grass, be sure to carry a stick with you. When the dog comes by, throw the stick and yell, "Fetch!" It works every time.

fact, grass is grown legally in Kentucky, but only by six farmers who are subsidized by the government (in order to keep a supply of hemp seeds around, in case somebody wants to make a rope or something). The hoe-downs in that part of the state are something else.

The first problem in growing grass, that of finding a suitable location, is relatively simple, but there are two risks one takes with whatever location he chooses: Having it found, which leads to being arrested, and having it found, which leads to it disappearing.

One good location is a distant field or an empty lot. The risk of arrest is greatly lessened here because all a person has to do is scatter some seeds in the chosen spot miles from his house, then cruise by that spot some three or four hundred times until the plants are mature, and, finally, cut them down at four-thirty one morning when there's a heavy fog and no moon. Since there is no proximity and only two moments of direct contact, the chance of being seen with the evidence is relatively slight.

However, the risk of having it lost is great. Unless your victory garden is truly secluded, other people may stumble upon it and clean you out a week before harvest time. Also, several animals (snails, rabbits, and certain dinosaurs) are singularly fond of young marijuana plants, and unattended fields of green are in constant jeopardy.

The risk of losing the grass, however, is greatly offset by the ease of planting it. You simply push some seeds into the ground about ¾ of an inch deep, and at least a foot apart, and get the hell out.

The other good location for planting seeds is in or around your own home. But here the risks and benefits mentioned above become reversed. That is, small risk from animals and people, but lots of risk from cops. For example:

YOU: But officer, it must've been my gardener who planted it.

OFFICER: Oh yeah? It was your gardener who tipped us off that it was here.

YOU: There's your proof. He's always hated me.

The only way you'll get out of this one is if you can prove that your gardener is a communist or gets a lot of speeding tickets.

Because the marijuana plant is so distinguishable, growing grass in your back yard or window box will very likely get you arrested unless you can camouflage or hide it for the four months it takes from germination till harvesting. Only you can determine whether the geography of your property will allow you to grow grass safely.

One method used by a friend of ours who shall remain nameless* was to label all the bushes, flowers and trees in his back yard including his marijuana plant, which he labeled "Cypress Tree." It didn't work.

The best results for growing it is to treat it like any other weed. Don't overly pamper it with fertilizers and scheduled waterings, or the plant will come to depend on constant attention. Remember, marijuana is the flower of love, but, like a seventeen-year-old girl, it gets emotionally involved too easily.

The seeds are extremely fertile, and if you plant a hundred seeds and give them at least partial sun and water, you will probably have eighty or ninety gorgeous young sprouts within three to four days.

Bird seed contains a certain percentage of grass seeds because the bird seed manufacturers' lobby was able to get an exemption from the law based on their claim that marijuana seed refurbishes the plumes of various birds. You probably have heard the apochryphal story of the little old gray-haired lady who was busted for having marijuana plants all over her back yard. Her defense was that she had an aviary there, and some of the seeds she threw to the birds must have sprouted. She was found guilty and is now serving ten years in jail (where she is known as "The Birdlady

* Fred Stimmons.

of Tehachapi") because the grass seeds in bird seed have been sterilized. Do you wonder what the man must be like who sits at a little bench all day sterilizing grass seed?

Marijuana is dioecious, as aren't we all, and thus has both male and female plants; but as they look very much alike and they both get you stoned (no matter what the folklorists say about only the female plant being potent), it doesn't matter which they are. Those who insist on only using the female plant probably have latent homosexual problems.

Be sure to have a stash around during the entire growth period, or you will bit by bit rape your garden, working from the bottom leaves up, until at the end of the growth period, all that will be left is a bunch of skinny stalks with teeny tiny flowers on it.

The leaves grow in odd numbers, with clusters of three near the bottom, then five higher up, and then seven. Some people have reported seeing nine and even eleven leaves in a cluster, but they may have been stoned at the time.

Leaves at the bottom will begin to shrivel and dry up as the plant adds sets of new leaves and grows taller. These you may pluck as they turn yellow, permit to dry, and then use. These leaves will probably give you an acceptable high, but one of very short duration. If you do pluck the leaves, trim off the stems. This will make the upper leaves more potent.

If you plant in April (probably the best time) you will harvest in late July or early August, at which time a myriad of pretty little ivory or purple or green-yellow flowers will adorn the tops of your now bushy and quite beautiful plants. You'll love them to death.

A few weeks before harvesting time, the air becomes filled with the excitement of all the villagers. On the day that the plants bloom, all the banks and schools are closed, and music echoes back from the hillside as the gaily dressed villagers begin cutting the plants down an inch above the soil.

The plants now are anywhere from five to twenty

feet tall. (The closer you plant the seeds, the shorter the plants will be. Warning: It's difficult to conceal a twenty foot marijuana tree.) They are then hung upside down on a clothesline, attached with clothespins or wire. Brew a mixture of sugar and water, boiling it until it thickens a little. Put the mixture in a Windex spray bottle or similar things, and spray the sugarwater all over the undersides of the plant's leaves (which will now be on top). Although this process is not mandatory, it causes the pollen (rich in resin) to adhere to the plant throughout the curing process, and guarantees optimum potency.

To cure, bundle the plants together, cover with a bag to collect those leaves which might fall, and leave in a dry hot place until the leaves crumble at the touch. A hot attic in late summer or a tent set up in a well sunlit place serves this purpose well. Curing may take another two weeks. If you're in a hurry, put the whole thing in the oven at 200 degrees for about fifteen minutes and do not bundle.

This method is not as good as the slow curing process—although no one knows this for certain, since no one that we ever heard of has used the slow cure process. Be very careful that you don't overcook it in the oven, because if you do it will be worthless for smoking, although it may still be perfect for eating.

After it's cured, remove the leaves, flowers, stems and seeds from the stalk, and throw the stalk away. In Chapter VI we discuss how to clean the grass.

RECEIVING GRASS AS A GIFT

Receiving grass as a gift is probably one of the nicest ways of all of acquiring it. Here are a number of methods which have stood the test of time:

Be very very nice to everyone, and keep reminding them of your birthday which is coming up next week.

Be a very beautiful girl with large breasts.

Look for people who are smoking pot, go over and stand next to them as quietly as possible, and look wistful. When they offer you a toke, be sure to say "Thank you."

Try to get on such programs as "Queen for a Day," or "My Secret Wish."

Whenever you take a walk, look on the ground for rolled up baggies with a rubberband around them.

Become a narcotics officer.

STEALING GRASS

This is the best of all. Sneak up behind someone and shout, "Hey, look up there!" When the unwary victim's attention is momentarily distracted, quickly steal all the grass he has on him and run away.

CHAPTER VI

Using Grass

Come up here, O dusty feet!
  Here is fairy bread to eat.
Here in my retiring room,
  Children, you may dine
On the golden smell of broom
  And the shade of pine;
And when you have eaten well,
Fairy stories hear and tell.

CLEANING

Normally, any quantity of grass you purchase from a
lid on up must be cleaned. It is, however, becoming
common to purchase a lid (in its characteristic wax
paper sandwich bag) which appears perfectly clean
and ready for use—but don't be fooled into thinking
you've made a great buy. All that may have happened
is that an unclean lid's worth was dumped into a
blender, including seeds, stems and roots, and maybe
pencil shavings and things from the floor, and then
around 80 % of that was sold to you. (After cleaning
an ounce, you usually have around 80% of the original
volume left.) Remember that the smaller the amount
you buy, the more you pay per X amount (or the
less you pay per Y amount if Y equals W over X
with W being any number handy). And if you buy
pre-cleaned grass, you will get less because the guy
who cleaned it usually will take some for his troubles.
It's always better to buy uncleaned grass, both because

of the above reasons and because the trash (stems, seeds, etc.) can be utilized in cooking.

If you did buy a clean lid and are curious about whether you've been taken or not, simply send it to us care of Random House or Dell or whoever winds up publishing this book, and we will write back giving you our opinion.

But for the moment, let us assume that you have a normal lid of uncleaned grass. You will now want to clean it. Empty the wax paper sandwich bag onto a sheet of newspaper and admire it. You will notice that what you have looks a lot like what might tumble out of a Lipton's orange pekoe and pekoe tea bag, only greener or grayer, with larger individual pieces, and with a great deal of light brown woody stuff, and a whole bunch of variously colored and shaped seeds. The strange papier-maché-like stuff which is clinging to the bigger pieces, and which crumbles when rubbed between the thumb and forefinger is what you're looking for. That's it. That's what the book is all about. That crumbly stuff is the dried leaves—the most potent part of the plant.

Simply stated, the purpose of cleaning grass is to separate the desirable dried leaves from the much less desirable stems and seeds. Later on, you can separate the seeds from the rest of the trash and plant them.

The reasons for cleaning grass become very apparent if you tried to roll a joint with uncleaned grass. The stiff stems will pierce the cigarette paper and make the whole thing unsmokable, and the seeds often explode upon contact with heat and things get into your eye or ignite your bedding or clothing. But it is just a teeny explosion, and rather pretty, so you may want to keep some seeds for smoking during Fourth of July.

If, however, you plan to smoke the grass in a pipe and therefore won't have any delicate paper to pierce and don't fear the teeny explosions, we still have to agree with a majority opinion that seeds and stems smoke much harsher and hotter than leaves. Just clean it and shut up.

There is one possible exception to cleaning the grass, and that is when you're going to use it for cooking. In cooking, all of the grass can be used. But because of a texture problem (the stems when chewed send the same chills down your back like when you accidentally chew sand in your tuna sandwich at the beach) you should make sure that everything is ground up into as fine a powder as possible in a blender. (See Tips On Cooking With Grass, page 150.) But if you're a purist, you'll have to remove the seeds and stems even if the grass is used for cooking, since they have little potency but do have flavor—unless you like the flavor, in which case you probably have emotional problems and we don't want to be bothered with you. Go eat stems and seeds and dirt and ants and filth; see if we care.

You may be wondering why we're messing around and haven't started telling you how to clean grass yet, even though that's the title of this part of the chapter. It's because we want the book to look fat so you think you're getting a lot for your $5.95 or dollar and a quarter or whatever you laid out for it. Which reminds us of a funny story that happened in Nebraska in 1948.

How to Clean Grass

Cleaning grass is so simple that we won't insult your intelligence by telling you how to do it.

NOTE: We've just received word from our publisher who said that if we don't tell you how to clean grass, there is no justification for this part of the book. We said, "The heck with you," and he said, "The heck with your book." So we said, "Okay, we'll tell how to clean grass," and he said, "Okay."

First, get a Grecian urn with various inscriptions on it by Keats, like, "Hail to thee, blithe spirit," or "God's in His heaven, all's right with the world." The inscriptions are for mood purposes. The urn must be exactly ten inches in diameter and no deeper than a foot. The colors should be bright and gay, but avoid puce and cerise, or people will talk.

Next, get a nine inch strainer or wire collander. The little krells on the side will fit neatly over the edge of the urn, and the strainer will nestle snugly into it.*

Next, get a wooden spoon made out of hickory.‡

Then get a table and a chair, or two chairs if someone is going to watch. And now you're ready.**

Break off a hunk of grass if you bought it in brick form, or throw in a whole lid. Take the spoon and stir the grass around in the strainer. The small pieces will fall through the holes in the strainer and into the urn, and the stems and seeds will stay in the strainer, unless you bought a strainer with holes that are too large. If you did, don't worry, nobody's perfect. Not even Sammy Davis, Jr.

As the contents of the strainer become more totally made up of the stems and seeds, begin picking up the stems and rubbing them between your thumb and forefinger over the strainer. This will loosen the tightly clinging dried leaves. Then continue the stirring procedure.

You'll find, as you continue with your work, that what you're doing, especially if you're stoned, is a creative and extremely magical occupation. There are many rewards involved in the process, such as every now and then lifting the strainer and looking into the urn to see how you're doing. If this is the case, you'll want to buy a second urn to dump the stripped stems and seeds into as you go along. A good idea is to get

---

* This is another glimpse of grass's notorious sexuality.
‡ Part of the spoon will grind off and get mixed with the grass, which will give the grass an outdoorsy flavor when smoked.
** In another chapter we examine the fact that routine processes take on exciting meanings and purposes if done while stoned. You may wish to apply that knowledge to this process.

matching urns, especially if you happen to be a matching urn freak.*

After about fifteen minutes of diligent work, you'll have a strainer or auxiliary urn full of seeds and stems, and a primary urn full of good clean grass.

Doctors and other rich people who have no appreciation for style and ritualism simply ignore the cleaning process as stated above and dump everything into a blender.‡ It works pretty well, but causes some serious problems with regard to the stems which we will ignore because those who clean grass with a blender are not our people.

All that's left now in terms of cleaning is to separate the seeds from the stems and plant the seeds in your next door neighbor's backyard.

The cleaning process described is to be used for no more than a quarter of a pound of grass at a time; therefore do this eight and a half times and you'll have a kilo cleaned.

Cleaning a kilo is obviously an overwhelming job and will take more than two hours. If you are cleaning a lot of kilos, the best thing is to use a wire brush and a piece of screening nailed to a bottomless wooden box—but this method isn't really that much better.

There are other methods which have been used to clean grass, such as using a flour sifter or a washing machine, but we believe that you'll find our method the best.

Improving The Quality Of Grass

Most of the grass found in the United States (the vast majority of which comes from Mexico) is not of good quality. In other words, one might have to

---

* For information about matching urns, send any amount of money over five dollars in stamps or coins to us, and we'll reply in some way eventually.

‡ Specialists and surgeons use only Osterizers with eleven buttons and use the liquefy button. GPs and Army doctors use a Kenmore with a Hi-Lo speed button.

smoke one, two, or even three joints in order to feel the effects to any enjoyable degree. Thus much activity and research has been done to find ways of improving poor grass, or of ways of making good grass even better. The human soul has always sought perfection.

Our friend Ernie Lundquist, in the American tradition of people like Edison, Pasteur and Curie, has devoted his life to making the world a more joyous place in which to live. Besides contributing to numerous charities, painting his sidewalk in various colors, and giving homes to stray dogs, girls and diseases, Ernie has worked night and day to find ways to perfect and improve the quality of grass. Unfortunately, he has failed completely. Below, however, is a list of ways which have been found to work.

Black Merta (sometimes called "Harold's Disease")

Take a lid or less of grass and put it into a one pound coffee can. Add enough water to make it soggy (one or two tablespoons) and put the plastic lid on tight. Bury the can about a foot in the ground (or in a dark damp corner of your basement or bedroom if you don't have any ground) and leave it there for at least a week. When you retrieve it, you'll discover that the grass is covered with a black weblike fungus. Dry the grass using a heat lamp (or any other method) and mix it all together. The grass will be at least twice as good, and probably better.

The Ice Pack Process

Get a thick cardboard box with a good lid and fill it with dry ice. Pour the loose grass (clean or unclean) into the box and cover it tightly. Depending on the outside temperature and how much dry ice you have, the ice should keep for a day or two. Keep the grass with the dry ice for at least 48 hours, but preferably longer. The ice does not become a liquid, but turns into gas; thus the grass should not get damp, although it might. If it does, dry it, of course. This method should cause the grass to be as much as five times better than it was.

If you can't get dry ice, dampen the grass and put it into a freezer. Leave it there for a week. Thaw and dry it. This method will improve it appreciably, but not as much as the dry ice process.

Ultra Violet Curing

Cure the grass which you've grown yourself under an ultra violet lamp instead of in the oven or under a heat lamp. This method takes about two weeks because the ultra violet lamp doesn't give off much heat. The only problem with this method is that after you smoke the grass you glow in the dark.

SMOKING GRASS

The Joint

By far the most common method of ingesting grass is to smoke it, and of all the smoking methods the most common is the grass cigarette, or joint, stick, number, Jay, or reefer. Hey, remember reefer?

A joint is simply grass rolled up in cigarette paper. The paper can be bought anywhere: markets, liquor stores, psychedelic shops, rodeos, or drugstores (that's interesting, when you think about it). An entire world of decisions can spring up about as simple a problem as which brand or type of paper to buy. There are dozens of brands, among which the most common are Bambu, Riz-La, OCB, Papel de Arroz, Blanco Y Negra, Papil de Hilo, Stella, LLF, Zig-Zag, Top, and Mafil. Interesting enough, Mafil spelled backwards is Lifam, and even more interesting, Lifam spelled backwards becomes Mafil again. And so on.

The types of papers are as varied as the brands.

There are small white papers, large white papers, brown papers, purple papers, licorice, strawberry and banana-flavored papers, heavily gummed papers, ungummed papers, newspapers, The National Review, and the Realist. And strange as it may appear, while the National Review and the Realist are entirely different, Paul Krasner and William F. Buckley, Jr. taste exactly the same.

The brand stocked by most stores throughout the country is Zig-Zag, which most people are thought to buy along with Bull Durham tobacco in a pouch. Bull Durham tobacco in a pouch comes with its own paper, but that paper is not gummed, so most people buy Zig-Zag paper for their Bull Durham tobacco in a pouch—or do they? Maybe they're really throwing away the Bull Durham tobacco in a pouch the moment they step outside the store. Maybe they're really buying the Zig-Zag paper for . . . other reasons?

The first time you buy Zig-Zag is very much like the first time you bought a little tin of three condums. You're nervous because that guy behind the counter knows that what you're about to do with what you just bought from him is a no-no. The only advantage to Zig-Zags over condums is that you don't get any more nervous if the person behind the counter is a woman.

The first time you buy Zig-Zag, therefore, you will probably also buy a pouch of Bull Durham tobacco because you're paranoid and insecure. You think that there are plainclothesmen hovering around liquor store counters who follow purchasers of Zig-Zag papers home and then bust in and arrest them. Well, it's true. All paranoid delusions involving grass are true. See? Now you'll never have to worry about being paranoid again.

And have you ever thought about that funny little liquor store clerk who sells Zig-Zag papers all day and never sells Bull Durham? What does he think is going on? And what about the Zig-Zag people themselves? What do they think? They must be richer than

Howard Hughes. Maybe they *are* Howard Hughes. By the way, we know a new Jane Russell story we'll have to tell you sometime.

So you buy the paper and scurry home, and get out the grass, and discover that you have absolutely no idea how to roll a joint properly.

How To Roll A Joint Properly

There are many ways to roll a joint, but we think that the method below is the easiest to explain and (because of the use of two papers instead of one) the easiest to roll and least likely to break or be pierced.

Take one sheet of cigarette paper and set it on a table so that the gummy side is at the top and facing you. Take a second sheet and lick the gummy edge, and then stick that edge face down to the bottom of the first sheet. You now have two cigarette papers stuck to each other. Wasn't that fun? Pick the whole thing up and fold toward you the bottom quarter of an inch or so. Open it and pour a little grass in the center of the crease and spread it out evenly along the full length except for the very ends. Close back the fold, trapping the grass in the crease, and tightly fold over the grass trapped section of the paper so that you have a firm bulge at the bottom. Then roll the bulge upwards between your thumb and first two fingers (with your thumb on top), keeping it tight, until you reach the gummy part, which you now lick and fold over. (If the gummy part isn't facing you when you get to it, you blew it.) Now lick the whole thing and fold over or twist each end tightly to keep the loose grass from falling out. And congratulations.

Cigarette tobacco contains potassium nitrate, an additive which keeps the tobacco from going out, and glycerin to keep it damp. Grass obviously does not have these additives, so your joint will probably go out often and will burn at least three times as fast as a cigarette. Lick the paper just before you smoke the joint, and this will retard the burning speed somewhat.

Different people roll different sized joints, depending on the kind of people they are, their rolling skills, and the amount of grass they have at the moment. Big fat joints are called Bombers or Thumbs. Very thin joints are called Very Thin Joints (although very thin people call them Pins).

You'll probably have to make a lot of joints before you get good at it, so don't get impatient. It's a safe bet that Joel McCrea and Randolph Scott could make great joints, but it probably took them at least three movies to learn.

There unquestionably will come the time when you want to roll a joint, but are out of paper. For the clever and ingenious, or for the dullards who were lucky enough to have bought this book, this will present no problem. Take a cigarette, plain or filter-tipped, and empty all the tobacco out of it except for the last quarter of an inch. The tobacco easily taps out after you have rolled the cigarette tightly between your thumb and forefinger. Fill up the now hollow tube of cigarette paper with grass, twirl the end, and you're home. But you must wet the paper even more than normally, because even though tobacco burns slower than grass, the paper around a ready-made cigarette burns much faster than the Zig-Zag kind. The reason for leaving a quarter inch of tobacco in the bottom is that you will thus avoid the problems of roach-smoking. Roaches will be covered fully later in this Chapter. Skip ahead if you have no self-restraint.

If you just happen to be out of papers *and* cigarettes, relax and grab a Tampax; take it out of the paper wrapper and fill the wrapper with grass. It works good. If you are concerned about what to do with all the unwrapped tampons lying around, simply freeze them for later use.

There is one other kind of joint which is clearly the most impressive joint possible; the ultimate. It's called the European or French joint. Few Americans mess with it or even know about it, but once you have rolled and tried a European joint, we can guarantee its place

in your rolling repertoire. (See Illustration) First
Step: Lay one sheet of cigarette paper on a table,
gummed edge up vertically on the left. Second Step:
Take a second sheet, moisten the gummed edge, and
put it *under* the first sheet, gummed edge up, along an
imaginary almost diagonal line running from the bottom left up to a half inch below the top right of the
first sheet. Step Three: Remove a filter from a filter
tipped cigarette, remove the paper around it, and lay
it on the bottom edge of the far right side of the second, or bottom, sheet. Step Four: Roll the paper
once around the filter, then, with one forefinger firmly
on the paper-covered filter, continue the rolling until
you have made a tube shaped like a megaphone. If

THE EUROPEAN JOINT

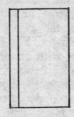

Step One

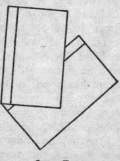

Step Two

you've rolled the paper around the filter tightly, its spongy quality will keep it well in place. Now moisten the gummed edge sealing the tube. Step Five: Pour four normal joints worth of grass in through the opening at the top and tamp it down with a cigarette or Q-Tip or something like that. Step Six: Fold the top edges inside the cone until the entire thing is solidly packed. You now have a European Joint.

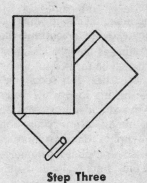

Step Three

Steps Four & Five

Step Six

Its unique qualities come from the conical shape, which permits an enormous area of grass to be lit and smoked while cooling it at the same time. You can even increase the effects of a European Joint (or any other joint) by smoking it as a Steamboat. Steamboats will be covered later in this Chapter. We see that you didn't skip ahead to Roaches before, and have thereby demonstrated your high degree of maturity and patience. Don't blow it by skipping ahead to Steamboats now.

Warning: If you get to be an expert at rolling joints, don't let anyone know. At first you'll enjoy the glory when everyone insists that you roll the joints, and then absolutely shine as they watch intently to see how you do it. You'll also be thrilled to discover that you're invited to all the parties. But soon you'll realize that everyone else is making love while you're sitting in a corner rolling your stupid joints. And one day, if you really get hung up on rolling your wonderful joints, you might look up to discover that everyone went down to the beach for nude swimming and left you behind, because they don't really like you.

Joint-Rolling Aids

Available to those among you who are hopeless klutzes are a great variety of inexpensive cigarette rolling machines, which take all the skill and creativity out of constructing a joint. The simplest and least expensive comes with Bambu paper, and, curiously enough, it's made of Bamboo. All it is is a thing that looks like a tiny bamboo window shade: It has a number of thick bamboo slats, one on top of another, connected by string at both ends. Just drop the grass along one of the bottom slats, lay the paper out evenly, fold the bottom of the bamboo roller up over the grass and keep on rolling till you feel a round tight cigarette inside. The first couple of times you do it, you will open the roller and find a tightly packed wad of grass lying on top of a scrunched up piece of paper, but after a while it comes easily and works very well.

Riz-La also makes a cigarette roller, which sells for from one to two dollars. It will roll a joint of any desired thickness, and you can even make filter-tipped joints with this gadget. It, too, takes a few tries out to master the technique, but it's worth it.

More sophisticated machinery exists and you who are acquisitionists will wallow in glory after you buy the machine that will roll a ten inch joint with the flick of a lever, then, if you wish, cut it into five regular-sized joints with another single motion.

The problem with most Rolling Gadgets is that they are bigger than a wallet, and thus not nearly as portable as some paper and your fingers. Also they lose their appeal after a week or two, and you will probably go back to the basic hand-made method except for party preparations, when you have to roll a dozen or more joints at a time. You'll also find that most cigarette rolling machines roll the joints a little fatter than you really want them.

The Roach

When you smoke a joint down to about the last half inch, you stumble upon a curious little thing called a roach, although sometimes it's called a cragzop.* Now, why is it called a Roach? Because by the time you smoke a joint down to the last half inch, it is stained brown and is generally icky, has two antennae, and when left in a lit room will scurry for cover in an old cupboard.

The Roach is a clumsy thing that should properly be thrown away, but, because of the cost, scarcity,

---

* Actually, it's never called a cragzop, but that sentence needed a little more rhythm—but why not call it a cragzop? If you do, people will say, "Hey, you must've read that book," and you'll say, "What book?" and a whole conversation will start which may develop into a meaningful relationship which will end in one of you getting hurt emotionally.

and dangers of acquiring grass, no one throws away nothing. So, various ingenious methods of consuming roaches have been devised.

Many people have taken to eating the roach. Often you'll hear conversations like this:

HE: What did you do with the roach?

SHE: I ate it.

HE: Oh.

Another method is that of making a cocktail. Take a regular kind of cigarette with printing on it and remove an inch of tobacco from one end. Drop the roach in, twirl the cigarette paper around it, wet the paper and light it. But the second you have smoked the cigarette past the roach, put it out. Cigarette smoking may be hazardous to your health.

A third method is to save up a whole bunch of roaches, empty the grass out and make another joint. Of course, when you smoke this joint, you will wind up with another roach, in which case you might want to use the fourth method.

The fourth method requires the use of a tool that will hold the roach so that your fingers won't get burned, which, we probably should have mentioned, is the main reason why roaches need four methods like these to smoke them.

(People rightfully worry about roaches lying around their house where they might be found the next day. We therefore have a fifth method which works when you're at someone else's house. Just say no when someone offers you a roach, pretending you've had enough. Eventually some mild-mannered self-effacing loser will do something with it, and a new joint will be lit.)

Getting back to the question of tools, a pair of tweezers works well, but you have to keep the pressure applied and in passing it someone usually drops the roach, thus burning the house down. A bobby pin or a springy hair clip (whatever they're called) works well, too, but nobody uses bobby pins anymore, except for a guy named Steve who identified with his mother when he was a kid and lives at the Y now. He can play Ping-Pong like you can't believe.

A very workable tool is a simple paper match. Split the match down the middle almost to the head, put the roach in between and hold the ends closed. This is called an airplane, or Jefferson Airplane, which probably answers a small question that has been nagging a lot of you for a while. The problem with this method is the same as that of the tweezers.

The best method is to purchase a roach holder or roach clip, and wear it around your neck where it'll always be handy. If anyone asks you what it is, tell them that you've just joined a new religion. If they continue asking about it, tell them that you're a Druid and that you've been washed in the blood of a tree. They'll soon go away.

The roach holder or clip is really nothing more than a tweezers in reverse, i.e. they're designed to stay closed unless pressure is put on them to open. These are euphemistically referred to as Philatelist Tongs at Psychedelic Shops, and they may range in cost from a dollar up to a hundred dollars for 18k gold creations rich in filigree. You might be interested to know that you can throw away at least two thousand roaches cheaper than buying an 18k gold roach holder, but, live and be well.

You can easily make your own roach holder by buying an alligator clip at a hardware or electronic store and welding it to the end of your finger.

Pipes

Any time you want to start an argument, you can bring up the question of the superiority of Pipes over joints, but as our President has asked us not to be divisive, we will not enter into the controversy.

The arguments in favor of the pipe are 1) there is nothing to construct and therefore no time is wasted doing monotonous tasks, 2) the lips come into contact with nothing unpleasant, 3) a considerable volume of smoke can be taken in with each puff, and 4) the smoke is greatly cooled (if the proper pipe is used).

The arguments in favor of the joint are 1) because grass burns so quickly, less is wasted in a joint, 2) pipes have to be cleaned every so often, otherwise there is a bitter taste, 3) they are more portable, and 4) they cost almost nothing.

If you do decide on a pipe, you must be sure that you purchase a proper one. Nothing is more gauche than smoking grass in an improper pipe. The standard college professor's briar pipe is typical of an improper pipe. It will work, obviously, but it's far outstripped by so many other kinds of pipes that anyone who buys a standard sized briar pipe for the purpose of smoking grass has made an unwise purchase. Not only will the grass burn too fast and too harsh, but the whole thing looks absurd. No, one does not want to look like a college professor while smoking grass; and if one *does* want to look like a college professor while smoking grass, it would be much more pleasant to simply sew leather patches on the elbows of one's sweater and sit around making seventeenth century puns.

The best normal type of pipe is one with a long stem and a bowl cover. The long stem not only helps to cool the smoke, but, when you pass it around, it makes you look and feel a lot like a Cherokee or some other kind of American Indian, thus assuaging some of your guilt feelings by replacing them with a general sense of being deprived and a mild resentment of the white man. The bowl cover will snuff the burning grass when you have had enough for a time, thereby eliminating waste, and at the same time it keeps the ashes from tipping out onto the bed.

The hookah or water pipe is perhaps the ultimate when it comes to cooling smoke, and if brandy or a wine with a heavy bouquet is used instead of the water, the taste is glorious.

Water pipes come in a myriad of styles, sizes and shapes, from tiny modern things that can be carried in a coat pocket, to Miltonic structures over six feet high. Multi-stemmed water pipes are obtainable, and the whole family can chug away simultaneously on these. If you do get a multi-stemmed pipe, make sure there are clamps or plugs on each stem to close it in case only one stem is being used.

One word of caution: Clean the stems and replace the liquid in your water pipe often, because when one gets fouled, it either blocks the smoke, or causes the vilest taste experience imaginable. However, do not entirely clean the ashes out of the bowl of a water pipe or any other kind of pipe. The ashes provide a further cooling filter, and without it the smoke can be exceedingly harsh no matter how nicely the pipe is designed.

There is one other kind of pipe, which many swear is the very best possible. It is called a table pipe in the pipe stores, and an air pipe by the heads. The one we've seen was made in Italy by Savinelli, whoever they are, and is called a "Kalumet." It's about three inches high and cone shaped. The top is two inches wide and the bottom is three inches wide, and it has a normal sized inner bowl. It's flat on the bottom, and there is a hole in the side to which a two foot flexible stem similar to those on hookahs is attached. The effect would appear to be that of a water pipe without the water, but the smoke is much cooler. It is apparent just how far into its infancy science still is, when you realize that it is unable to explain this phenomenon.

There are many variations on the three above mentioned types of pipes, and you may want to browse among these at a Pipe Shop or Psychedelic Shop. Your inevitable choice will have to boil down to a matter of visual aesthetics since neither Pipe Shops nor Psychedelic Shops will permit you to test puff a pipe. And if they will, inform them that they're breaking various Health and Safety Codes, and attempt to make a citizen's arrest.

Homemade Pipes

A fun thing to do on a wintry evening is to make your own water pipe. It's cheap and simple, and it answers the question of what to do with the empty wine bottle that has the hole in the side for ice and the tassle and everything, or the bottle with the candle in it that you've been melting crayons over whenever you were depressed.

For complete instructions on how to build one, see page 132.

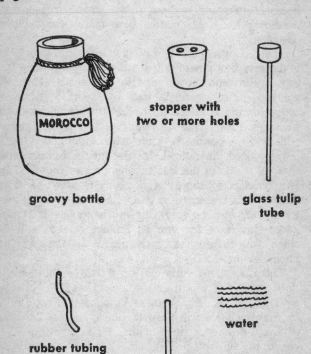

groovy bottle

stopper with two or more holes

glass tulip tube

rubber tubing one or more

water

glass "Y"
tube
(optional)

clamps — one
for each
rubber tube

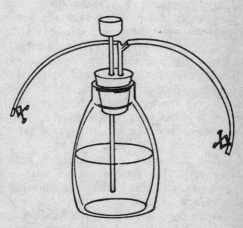

Homemade water pipe

The glass tulip tube will hold the grass with very little loss, although you might want to add a piece of screen or strainer. Make sure that this tube goes well into the water, so that the water can filter the smoke. All the above components can be bought in a chemical supply store for less than $2.00 (not counting the bottle). For one smoking stem, you need a two hole stopper and a glass tube. For two smoking stems, you need a stopper with three holes, or two holes and a "Y" tube. If the bottle is transparent, you can easily tell when the pipe has gone out, because if it has the smoke in the bottle will clear with one puff.

The Tandyn Slave-Master

The most perfect device in all the world ever invented for the smoking of grass is a thing we've called the "Tandyn Slave-Master," which was invented by Tandyn Almer, the same person who wrote the words and music to the hit song, "Along Comes Mary." (It's interesting to note that anyone who is good in one area is usually good in other areas. Tandyn is not only a successful composer, poet and inventor, but he's brilliant with a sewing machine, lives with a beautiful movie star, and can tap dance like a son of a bitch.*)

Every device used for smoking grass has the one problem of wastage. No matter how fast you smoke it, about half of the smoke is dissipated into the air, and thus lost forever. The Tandyn Slave-Master, however, has done away with this problem by allowing you to save every bit of the smoke.

The reason for the name "Slave-Master" is that it takes two people to operate it; one does the work and the other reaps the benefits (just like in a marriage). Although this device can be easily and cheaply built,

---

* Ernie hates him.

it is a little complicated to explain, so please refer to the illustrations on pages 134-135.

On the left is a normal water pipe such as the one we've just described, except that it is connected by a glass or rubber tube to the incinerator on the right.

Grass is placed into a heat-proof flask (which we'll call the incinerator) and stopped up with a two hole stopper. The incinerator is placed on a stand and a Bunson burner or can of sterno (or gas range) is placed under it. Two tubes are connected to the two hole stopper; one hangs free and the other goes to the water pipe.

When the grass begins to smolder, one person (the "slave") blows into the free hanging incinerator tube. His air goes into the incinerator forcing that air out into the other tube. The air from the incinerator contains very hot and potent smoke from the smoldering grass. This smoke goes through the incinerator's exiting tube and into the water in the water pipe where it is cooled. The smoke then goes to the top of the water pipe and pours out of the exiting tube and into the mouth of the second person (or "master").

When you've had enough and the slave and the master have changed places (which is the American way) then remove the heat source and let the slave blow air into the incinerator until all the smoke has come out of the water pipe's existing tube.

One last note, clamp the water pipe and the incinerator together in order to keep them from tipping over. You can build the Tandyn Slave-Master for about eight dollars.

Steamboats

The Steamboat is a combination of a pipe and a joint merging the best of both into a powerful tool of good. It's usually made from a cardboard tube, such

THE TANDYN SLAVE-MASTER

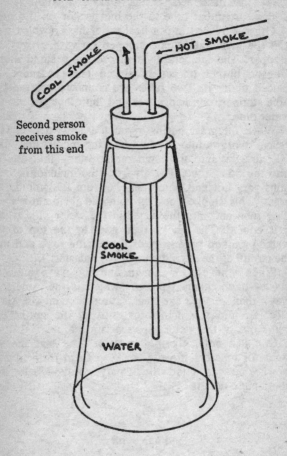

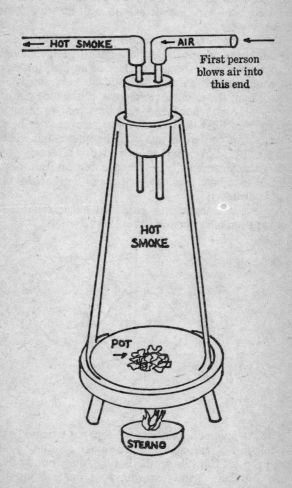

as the kind you find when you've used up a roll of toilet paper or paper towels. The technical name for these cardboard tubes is "Der-der." It got this name because when you were a kid you put it to your mouth and said "der-der" into it as you walked around the house.

To make a Steamboat simply poke a small hole in the tube near one end. The hold must be large enough to squeeze a joint about a quarter of an inch through, but small enough so that the joint fits very snugly.

Now light the joint, cover the end of the tube closest to the joint with one hand, and draw smoke through the other end. At the last moment, remove your hand —this allows cool air to mix with the smoke. Incredible volumes of smoke can be extracted with each puff through a Steamboat, and when a big fat European Joint is used, the results would make Zeus shake his head in disbelief.

A glass steamboat with an added phenomenal feature has been manufactured, and looks like this:

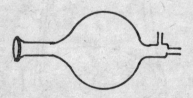

You simply put a joint into the top, put a finger over the hole in the rear, and puff. No smoke goes into your mouth; instead, it fills up the bottle. After four or five puffs, you puff again removing your finger from the posterior hole. A horrendous amount of cool smoke is taken in, and it's probably all you'll need for the night.

There are a number of variations of Steamboats to be found at this writing, but we feel that the Art of the Steamboat is still primitive. Oh, to be imbued with immortality so as to witness the future wonders of Steamboatdom!

Here are two noteworthy variations:

Take a piece of bamboo about a foot long, and dig a hole near one end. Insert the stem and bowl of a pipe, after having removed the mouthpiece. You smoke it holding the bamboo vertically, opening and closing the bottom hole. While smoking it you can pretend to be Earl Bostig.

Take a paper towel der-der, and make two holes in it; one an inch from the end, and the other two inches from the end. Buy two metal thimbles and, with a hammer and nail, make little holes in the bottom. Insert the thimbles into the holes of the der-der and fill each with grass.

Some inveterate critics may claim that these are not Steamboats, but pipes. They're not. They're Steamboats. A pipe has two holes, a Steamboat three or more.

Smoking Paraphernalia

Paraphernalia range from the previously mentioned roach holders to the New York Philharmonic. There are so many wondrous things you can buy to enhance your smoking pleasure that a sojourn through a really good Psychedelic Shop can be an experience ranging from giddy to deeply moving. However, see Chapter 1 for the dangers of going into a Psychedelic Store while stoned.

One of the good things that these stores carry, and that you should buy, is incense (although religious stores of a Christian nature usually have a better selection). There are many different fragrances (e.g. Sandalwood, Jasmine, Rose, Liver, Chicken, and Cheese), and each serves the purpose that God intended incense for: that of masking the sweet sickening smell of grass.*

You may well ask, "Why mask the smell of grass?" The answer is in case your mother or father, or son or daughter, comes home early.

Of all the incense fragrances, we most strongly recommend Sandalwood, since it does seem to cut through the grass smell best, and has a very pleasant odor. But don't go by us.

Incense also comes in different shapes, such as sticks, cubes, and pyramids, but the best comes in powdered form in a little box which also contains a little metal device that picks it up and puts it into pyramid form. The box costs about 50¢ and it lasts longer and smells stronger. Of course, now you've got to buy an incense burner, and we can see where this whole thing is beginning to cost a fortune.

The Art Of Smoking

There is no pretense or status seeking when it comes to smoking grass. The object is to get stoned, and all other values are seldom if ever discussed, as is the case with liquor. When we drink booze, we lie and mess around. We make great fusses over the superior flavor of scotch to bourbon, Chivas Regal to Vat 69, Crown Royal to Canadian Club. This is perhaps the one area of mystique to which drinkers can lay claim. Ironically, it is a sham. Granting the possible exception of a Tom Collins on a sweaty ninety degree day, any honest person would have to admit that any soft drink tastes better than any hard drink. Even that Tom Collins tastes better with the gin left out. And after the

---

* Grass' odor is neither sweet nor sickening, but no one ever describes it in any other way, and since this is our first major published work, we dared not be different. In our second major published work, called *We Dare To Be Different*, we shall describe how grass really smells, as well as let you know once and for all whether Rock Hudson is what everyone says he is.

first drink, your taste buds are so dulled that you can't tell one brand from the next (even blindfolded).

With grass there are only two qualitative considerations: It is so harsh that you choke and wretch with every puff, and does it get you stoned? Since the sections on smoking devices and cleaning adequately dismissed the problems of harshness, all that remains is how to get higher faster.

Before we get to that, though, (patience is the winged chariot that brings the golden sun to the midnight cold—Ernie Lundquist, 1964). we should explore the relative merits of different kinds of grass.

There are various breeds of grass, with the most familiar being Acapulco Gold, Panama Red, Chicago Green, and Mexican Blue Dirt Grass. For years the best has been considered to be Acapulco Gold, although there are two new breeds floating around which are far superior.

Ice Pack (or Ice Bag) came into Los Angeles sometime in 1966, and was very expensive. While most grass in Los Angeles sells for $100.00 a kilo, with Acapulco Gold going for around $200.00, Ice Pack was selling for $300.00. The effects were supposed to be three or four times that of normal good grass.

It seems that Ice Pack is sometimes known as Michoacan (which is a state in Mexico). There are two well known and conflicting stories regarding this grass. One is that the grass was smuggled in inside crates of frozen lettuce (hence Ice Pack). The other is that a famous L.A. disk jockey had two tons of the stuff brought in on a Navy mine sweeper in huge drums. He is not on the air anymore, and is believed to be in Europe with a lot of money.

The other breed is said to have an effect close to that of LSD, although this is doubtful. It's called Purple Seedless, and, because no one seems to have had more than just a taste, little is known about it, except that it had no seeds.

It's possible that Purple Seedless is the same as Ice Pack because Ice Pack had no stems and almost no seeds. It seems that everyone has a different story about grass involving an unusual name and exaggerated potency.

Due to different climates, soil conditions, and mixtures of top and bottom leaves, there is no question that grass differs in degrees of potency, even within the same breeds. But, is there a different effect induced by different kinds of grass? Is there depressing grass, eating grass, horny grass, talking grass? It's our contention, although there seems to be no way to prove it, that there isn't any correlation between mood and specific grass—it just depends on the mood you're in when you start smoking, or the mood you get into after you're stoned. What seems to happen is that a person buys a lid, tries it, and finds himself laughing a lot. He then exclaims, "Hey, this is laughing grass!" and forever more, whenever he uses that grass, he finds himself laughing.

Getting back to the question of how do you get stoned faster, how do you get stoned faster? Well, aside from using the right grass and the different devices mentioned earlier, there is the fine practice of hyperventilation.

Little hyperventilation is simply taking in a mixture of air with the smoke. It's a quasi-artificial high and a temporary one that hangs on till the full high of the grass takes over, but there is much to be said for it. Instead of smoking a joint the way you smoke a cigarette (lips tightly wrapped around it), open the lips slightly and suck in air without direct contact with the joint. The smoke will still come, but with a good deal of air mixed in. (This also helps to cool the smoke.) After merely a puff or two, you will begin to feel the lightheadedness that comes after blowing up a balloon. Some people who place greater emphasis on smoking style than is really necessary will take a drag in this manner, hold it in, then place the burning end of the joint near their lips and suck in the smoke that rises from it. This is sort of silly but it looks like they know what they're doing.

Hyperventilation smoking is more difficult with a pipe, but still can be accomplished in approximately the same manner.

Big hyperventilation is a much different process, and the result gives you a fantastically intense high that lasts for about 10 to 20 seconds, but which could seem like hours. The process is exactly the same as what you used to do when you were ten, only then it made you dizzy and sometimes you fainted. However, if you're stoned and you do this, you won't faint; instead, you'll be transported.

After becoming well stoned, crouch down on your knees. Take five slow very deep breaths and hold the last one. Stand up, put your thumb in your mouth and blow very hard, but don't let any air out. Blow until you feel a slight pressure in your forehead, then stop. A few seconds later, you start soaring very high, reach a plateau, and then come down.

It's advisable to have someone hold you when you do this, as you don't want to be bothered with trying to stand up. Sometimes four people will do this together and support each other.

A mild variation of this is after taking a deep puff of smoke, put your thumb in your mouth and blow without letting any air out. You will feel a tiny poignant high, and sometimes little spiral-like feelings will shoot up inside your head.

There really isn't much to say about how to smoke in order to get higher, except for the methods we've discussed. If it's your first or even second time, don't expect much (but be sure to see Chapter 1 where we talk about the problems of first time smokers).

In normal grass smoking, inhale deeply and hold it in as long as you can before you exhale. If this doesn't work, smoke more. If this still doesn't work, see the section on cooking. And if this still doesn't work, take the book back and try and get your money refunded.

Getting as high as possible is not always the aim in smoking grass as well as in drinking. For many things, such as reading, you should not have more than a very mild high. If you get too high, reading becomes impossible. It becomes something like reading the news on the old Times Building in New York, if it were to go in slow motion. You forget the beginning of the sentence by the time you get to the end. If you try to read while very stoned, you'll find that you're reading the same paragraph over and over, trying to get it to make sense. This is not necessarily a bad practice, though, as it cuts down on your cost of books. Our friend Ernie has been reading *Moby Dick* for the last three months. So far he's gotten as far as "Call Me Ishmael," at which point he breaks into hysterics, forgets what he just read, and starts over.

Very often you'll find yourself in the company of someone who has never turned on before, but who also doesn't smoke. You're then faced with the hassle of having to teach them to inhale. There is, however, an easier way, a way known as the Blowgun Method. Simply get a straw, take a puff, inhale, and blow the smoke out through the straw into the non-inhaler's mouth while they breathe in. (This method is the absolutely best method for cooling the smoke. The millions of capillaries of your lungs filter the smoke and make it mild, without removing very much of the potency.) The smoke will go into the other person's mouth in a narrow stream, and he or she will not feel the smoke whatsoever.

If you are using a pipe, and don't have a straw, you can achieve somewhat the same effect by aiming the stem at the person's mouth and blowing into the bowl.

To some extent you can use the Blowgun Method without the straw or pipe by touching lips with the other person and blowing. This is a Good Thing To Do if they're a member of the opposite sex. If they're a member of the same sex, shame on you.

An interesting note about smoking grass—almost everyone reports that the more they smoke grass, the less they need to get high. When they first started smoking it, it may have taken two or even three joints to get high, whereas after a year of moderate use, it only takes one or even one half to get high. This seems to be the reverse of drugs, which are almost all tolerance building. Weird.

Of all the methods of ingesting grass, smoking is by far the most common because of the need for a minimum of preparation. A little grass, a sheet of cigarette paper, and some fire, and you can be stoned. The second major advantage of smoking over the other methods of ingesting is the speed with which one gets stoned, but just exactly how fast varies with the individual smoker.*

EATING GRASS

Don't eat raw grass if you want to get stoned. Eat raw grass if you want to get sick. Raw grass does not get you stoned no matter how much you eat, and no matter what anybody says. It has to be cooked in some way first. We don't know why; we're reporters, not philosophers.

Eating cooked grass is absolutely and unequivocally the best way to use grass! We probably just lost half the heads who are reading this, but we resolutely stick by that statement. Eating cooked grass is the easiest way of getting stoned and it gets you much more stoned and keeps you stoned much longer than does smoking or any other way. There is no tell-tale odor to be reckoned with, there is no harsh burning to your throat and lungs, and you never cough, and if a sudden knock cometh at your door, you can devour the evidence with pleasure.

Setting aside the argument of the impulse convenience of smoking, the only qualitative factor of smoking over cooking is that smoking gets you high faster. And if you must get high that fast, you probably use the

---

* Our friend Ernie claims that he gets high on a single puff. Ironically, he also claims his Volkswagen gets 43 miles per gallon of gasoline.

grass because of a whole bunch of wrong reasons and should immediately become an alcoholic.

There are also times when you may want to combine both methods. For example, if you were going to see "2001, A Space Odyssey," the first big-screen trip movie ever made, you would want to be stoned for the light show part of it, which comes almost three hours after the film begins. But you usually are coming down after three hours, and it's not cool to smoke a joint during intermission. So you smoke just before leaving the house (that way you're stoned for the beginning of the film) and you eat some brownies after the first hour in. The brownies take effect in the second hour, and by the third hour you're in good shape.

It takes approximately one hour before any real effect takes place after you've eaten grass in a recipe. With some individuals it often takes as long as two hours and with others as short a time as twenty minutes to reach a definite and total stoned condition.*

The problem is clearly a matter of how long it takes the digestive system to permit the grass resin to take effect. So doubling or tripling the amount of grass in a recipe is foolhardy and brazen, although it will permit you to serve smaller pieces of whatever it is you will be cooking.

We should again stress the fact that you usually don't feel the effects of grass after you've eaten it for a good hour. Many times at a party some of the guests will want more brownies after a half hour, because nothing is happening. Keep them away from it. Although there is probably no such thing as a lethal dose‡ a large amount does cause drowsiness.

* Our friend Ernie claims that it takes him only three minutes after eating grass to get stoned. Ironically, he can also make love for seven and a half hours.
‡ According to a recent experiment reported in *Time* magazine, the amount needed to kill a mouse is 40,000 times the amount it takes to make a man high, so one might assume a lethal dose for a man might be to eat 100 pounds of grass all at once.

The first time our friend Ernie ate grass, he didn't feel the effects until after leaving the party (almost two hours later) and he thought it didn't work. He started to drive from the party (in Hollywood) to his home (in Westwood) and ended up in Santa Barbara (90 miles away). He said that driving was such a gas that he couldn't stop. Ernie is well aware that driving while stoned is dangerous, but you know Ernie.

There is only one risk in cooking with grass, and that is not using enough. It usually takes a great deal of grass to even begin to think about making some kind of taste treat. Don't think about it unless you have a spare lid lying around somewhere. Nothing is more frustrating than throwing a half a lid into a brownie recipe and not having enough to get the whole gang stoned.*

As a general rule, one lid of grass used in cooking will get twenty people very high or one person very high twenty times, or if one person eats the entire recipe all at once, he should not be expected to show up for work or his mommy's house for a long long time.

A point we've made before is that grass is not among the most tasty substances around. The flavor resembles some spice that found its way into a particularly bad Slavic soup, and its texture lies somewhere between pumice and a good grade of sawdust. Each recipe was carefully chosen, therefore, to hide the flavor and texture of the grass as much as possible, and several dishes manage their task completely. One even tastes better with grass in it than without. Let's see if you can guess which one it is.

---

* Actually, there are two things that are even more frustrating. One is to have enough to get everyone in the gang stoned except you, and the other is to get everyone in the gang stoned including you, and then realize that they're all guys. Of course, if you really want to get into this, the thing that is the most frustrating of all is getting a corn kernel stuck between your teeth. See our new book, *1001 Dental Jokes.*

Cooking With Grass

Table Of Measurements For Raw Cleaned Grass

    1 oz. = one Spice Island spice jar
    1 oz. = ½ cup
    1 oz. = 8 level tablespoons
    1 oz. = 24 level teaspoons
    1 level tablespoon = 3 level teaspoons
    1 level teaspoon = one good joint or two average joints

Tips On Cooking With Grass

The spoons in your silverware drawer are usually shallower than regulation measuring spoons, and probably hold about half the volume. Figure that one heaping teaspoon is easily equal to one good portion.

The more you grind the grass, using a blender or pressing it through a very fine strainer, the less gritty the dish will be.

If you use grass in a cake recipe, be sure to add more liquid or eggs, because the grass will make the cake much heavier than normal.

When cooking with grass, always try to pick a recipe that is very spicy or which contains foods with a heavy flavor, in order to mask the terrible taste of the grass. And never use monosodium glutamate (MSG or Accent) because it brings out the grass flavor.

We do not recommend that you boil grass because the boiling seems to cut down on the potency tremendously. When you boil grass, the house will reek with the odor for days, and this is probably where all the potency has gone. Frying, baking, broiling, or roasting grass is fine, but boiling should be used only for the debris (seeds, stems and stalks) which is usually thrown away anyway. (It should be noted that some people report that seeds make them slightly sick, but these people are in the minority.)

Elixir

If you want to do the best job possible in terms of removing the texture and taste problems, we urge you to use the following method to make a kind of "elixir."

Take the amount of grass which you're going to use and put it into a dry frying pan. Fry the grass over a low to medium fire for about five minutes, stirring it to make sure that it doesn't burn. It is done when it begins to turn brown and wisps of smoke appear. Let it cool for a few minutes, and grind it into a powder with a mortar and pestle (or a wooden spoon and bowl).

The elixir is ready to be eaten at this point, and you can do anything you want with it: Put it into jello, ice cream, peanut butter, milk shakes, or anything else which doesn't require cooking. You can even put it into a salt shaker and sprinkle it on anything.

For taste purposes it is still better to put it into a recipe (it will not lose its potency even though it's cooked again).

If you prepare the grass in this manner, the need for specific recipes is obviated. We will include a few recipes however, because they are of special interest.

Recipes

HONEY SLIDES

This is the fastest and most palatable method of eating grass. You will thank us for this recipe a hundred times over.

> 1 heaping teaspoon of grass
> 2 or 3 tablespoons of honey

Fry the grass as if you were making the elixir, but you don't have to grind it. Heat the honey (important). While the honey is still warm, add the fried grass and mix it well. The honey completely coats the grass, and when you eat it it just slides down your throat. Serves one.

COP-OUT BROWNIES (using package mix)

We include this recipe because it has become the traditional method of cooking with grass in the United States.

> 1 16-oz. package of Betty Crocker Fudge Brownie Mix
> ½ cup of grass
> 2 eggs
> ½ cup of nuts or ground macaroons

Follow the directions on the box for cake-like brownies rather than the fudge brownies. We recommend Betty Crocker Mix because it has the strongest brownie flavor and thus best masks the grass flavor. Put the raw grass in a bowl and mix it well with the dry brownie mix. Add the water and the two eggs, and mix. You might find that you have to add about another teaspoon of water. Add the nuts or macaroons (this is used to camouflage the gritty grass texture). After cooling, cut into twenty portions. Put each portion into a separate baggie and store in freezer. They can be eaten frozen. If you are going to eat all of them within a week, you don't have to freeze them, of course.

BUTTER

This method of making butter is called for in the recipe for the famous White Cooky of Marrakesh, but, of course, it can be used in the cooking of anything. If it is made carefully, the final dish in which the butter is used will be odorless and tasteless in terms of the grass.

2 or more cups of debris
2 quarts of water
1 lb. of butter

Heat the water to full boil and add the debris and butter. (You could, of course, use clean grass, but you would be wasting it.) Let the water come to a boil again and then simmer for six hours covered. Don't take the cover off too often, but stir it occasionally and don't let all the water boil out. Add more water if necessary. Pour all of the mixture through a cheesecloth or an extremely fine strainer, and squeeze out all the liquid from the pulp. Put the pulp in a cup of boiling water, and strain again. Throw the pulp away. Put the liquid in the refrigerator over night, where it will solidify. Pour out any remaining liquid. It is difficult to tell how potent the butter will be because it depends on the quality and quantity of debris used. You'll have to experiment. For garlic butter, add six cloves of garlic to the boiling mixture about three hours in.

TEA

"Fraud Tea"

Add one level tablespoon of grass to one cup of boiling hot water. Let set for 3 minutes. Drink. Nothing happens. People insist that this works, but our testing laboratory reports negative.

"Terrible Tea"

2 cups of water
3 heaping tablespoons grass

Boil covered for one hour. Drink. Vomit. Very mild high.

NOTE: Scientists have made an extract of the essence of grass called tetrahydracanabinol (THC).

Drinking a little bit of it gets you stoned. It is obvious that the scientists did not simply boil the grass.

MISCELLANEOUS FORMS OF INGESTION

Osmosis

We have come across instructions which claim that if you mix grass with sunflower seeds, garlic, chicken fat and some other stuff, and rub it all over your body, you'll get high, but nobody we know has tried it and who cares.

Suppositories

Two methods still in the experimental stage are enemas and suppositories. We asked an anal compulsive friend of ours to aid us in our research, but he just looked confused and started emptying ash trays.

Contact High

When someone is in a room with one or more people who are smoking, and that person can't or won't smoke, he'll often get very high merely by the superfluity of the smoke in the air. Many people turn on for the first time this way without knowing it.

Many people use the term Contact High to mean that someone is with others who are high will start to act high too, although there is no smoke around. Both of these uses of the term are probably correct. What do we know?

CHAPTER VII

Stashing Grass

When I am grown to man's estate
I shall be very proud and great,
And tell the other girls and boys
Not to meddle with my toys.

IN GENERAL

Now you've progressed to the point where you find yourself with a bevy of grass lying around. What if the meter man sees it? What will he think of you? It's apparent that you can't just leave it on the coffee table, although Agatha Christie once had one of her characters leave an important piece of evidence lying in plain sight. The police never found it because, of course, the police never look in obvious places. Maybe it wasn't Agatha Christie. Who can remember such things?

Maybe it was Erle Stanley Gardner? Forget it.

If you buy a large amount, a kilo or a pound, bury it in a tightly sealed container, after having removed a month's supply. Probably an ounce will be enough. Okay, where do you hide the ounce?

The first requirement is that you pick a specific place and keep it in only that place. If you put the unused part away just anywhere while you're stoned, you may forget where you put it, or even that you had some left over. After a while you may end up with six or seven little stashes all over the house, which no one, including you, knows about. This is wasteful and dangerous.

The second requirement is that the place you pick must be easily accessible. If it isn't, you won't put it away after using it. You'll just leave it lying around, believing that you'll put it away tomorrow. Unfortunately you don't remember or notice it, and it sits on the coffee table for a week.

The last requirement is that it be a place which no one is liable to accidentally stumble upon.

HIDING PLACES

The Spice Rack Ploy

Because an ounce just about fills a spice jar, many people put it in a spice jar. Now you're standing there with a spice jar filled with grass, and the idea flashes through your mind with the cataclysmic force of pure raw creative energy, "Put it in the spice rack!" So you label it "oregano," which it looks and feels like, and you put it in the spice rack. Then you step back and admire your work, your little chest puffed out in pride at your great ability as a problem solver (little realizing that a racoon solved this same problem in a minute forty-five seconds—although it did take a horse almost a half hour.

Well, you did a dumb thing. First of all, unless you look very Italian, the fact that you have two spice jars filled with oregano is going to seem very suspicious. The second bad thing is that in every narcotics raid, one officer is assigned to go immediately to the spice rack and sample the oregano.

If, because of some private neurotic obsession, you have to put it in the spice rack, put it in a pepper can first. Nobody would ever think of looking there.

Our friend Ernie Lundquist once came up with a good idea. He ground up the grass until it was very fine, then he soaked it in red vegetable dye and mixed it with a little paprika. His idea was to put it in a spice jar labeled "paprika." The only problem was that it wouldn't dry. After about a week of having a dish of soggy red grass and paprika lying around, he popped it into the oven. In fifteen minutes it developed a golden brown crust and tasted just like chicken.

The Hollow Book Ploy

Hollowing out a book is not a bad idea. It's worked for hundreds of years. Everybody knows how successful it is, even the police (except for a Patrolman Novashampski, of the LAPD, who can't read). So when they bust in, they start going through all your books, ususally dropping them on the floor. If you're not worried about the police and just don't want guests to notice the pot, then a hollow book is excellent. But be sure you get the correct book.

Esoteric books are out, because one of your guests is sure to have gone to junior college and makes it a point of looking over everybody's books to show that he's interested in such things. And if he got good grades, he's sure to want to thumb through *Simplified Serbo-Croation,* or *A Non-Euclidian Examination of Sponges and Coelenterates.* Nothing in this area is safe. Our friend Ernie once caught his milkman looking in *A View of Lambert's Notes on Ingersoll.*

Absolutely avoid any book that even implies that a reference to sex might be contained within. *An Illustrated Guide to Modern Canadian Sex Practices* is sure to be opened by everyone.

Curio books should be avoided because most people are at least momentarily intrigued by such things. One out of seven people will look through *A Book of Watches,* and one out of four will look at *The Pullman Car.*

Because of the nostalgia factor, avoid all children's books, even *Mr. Wipple's Aeroplane,* or *Freddy Meets the Ignoramus.*

Combination books should be passed over because they attract attention. Never hollow out *The Telephone and the Spanish Inquisition,* or *The Bobbsey Twins Go To A Foot Fetish Party.*

And, finally, avoid all reference books. One day some very straight Junior High School Social Studies teacher that your aunt fixed you up with is going to want to look up something to prove some point she's making, and you know very well it'll get back to your whole family. The best thing to do with this kind of girl is tell her you've got the clap and get her the hell home fast.

By and large, obscure fiction is the best. Our friend Ernie hollowed out *The House Near The Stream,* by Ruth Erlich, and it worked good for a whole year. But, unfortunately, Ruth Erlich came by one day and, well, you know the rest.

The Hollow Door Ploy

This is an excellent idea, but it takes work. All you need is a wood chisel, a hammer, and a chair. Carefully dig into the top of a door (making sure it isn't one of those modern hollow doors) and remove a half inch wide by four inches long by one inch deep slab. Then dig down another five inches, but leave a ledge of ½ inch on either side. The slab will fit neatly back, and you've got a space three inches long, five inches deep, and ½ inch wide. Put your grass in a baggie and hide it in the secret hollowed door. You should be able to keep about an ounce there.

The Shower Curtain Rod Gambit

The hollow shower curtain rod is one of the places that is certain to occur to you, but it's a bad idea because the screws that go into the wall eventually widen the holes through constant screwing and unscrewing. Also, the grass, one day, will slip into the rod much farther than your fingers can reach, and the whole thing becomes stupid.

The Cake Box Shuck

Bake a cake with a lid of grass in it (see recipes, page 152). Go to the store and buy a cake with a well known brand name on the box. Take it home, throw away the cake, and put your cake with the grass in it into the box. If the police search your house and find it, let them arrest the bakery. If they search your house and don't find it, don't offer them some cake and milk before they leave.

HIDING PLACES TO AVOID

The Hollow Chair Leg

The chair will break when a cop is over asking about the man who used to live next door.

Taping It Under Things

The tape loses its stickum and you have to keep getting new tape. Sometime, during a humid day, when your minister has brought over the church choir to meet you, the tape will loosen and the grass will fall on the floor with a huge noise.

Putting the Grass In A Small Jar And Putting That Jar In A Large Jar Of Mayonnaise

You get mayonnaise on your hands and in your hair and everything.

Throwing It Way Up High

Excellent, for very short periods of time.

Putting It In The Radiator

Not so good in the winter.

Putting It In The Oven

Okay, but be careful during the Pillsbury Bake-Off season.

As a tip, don't use anything we've mentioned in this book because now everybody will know about these places.

And here's a warning: Don't tell anybody where it's hidden. Nobody. Hide it in a place where you can get to it with nobody seeing where it is, even though a party is going on in your house at the time.

We can't stress enough your not telling anybody. Here's a true story for your reading enjoyment:

Norman was a big pusher, of a lot of things, and he came up with the following idea: He rented apartment #22, and had a friend rent the apartment next door, #23, for him. Norman lived in #22, and he kept his stash in #23, which he fixed up to look lived in, in case the manager went in (to "look for gas leaks").

When Norman went to make a sale, he picked up the stuff from #23 and delivered it. He figured, and rightly so, that if the cops got wind of him and got a warrant to search his apartment, they'd find nothing.

Norman was so proud of his plan that he told some of his closest friends. Unfortunately, one of his closest friends was an undercover cop who'd been with him for three months. When the police busted into his house with a warrant to search #22, they also had a warrant for #23. Norman is now in jail.

Don't use a "friend's" plan, and don't tell anyone your plan. The life of crime is a lonely life.

The Dangers of Grass

A child should always say what's true
And speak when he is spoken to,
And behave mannerly at table;
At least as far as he is able.

The dangers of using grass are:

1)—Getting busted.

The Morality of Marijuana

A Birdie with a yellow bill
Hopped upon the window sill,
Cocked his shining eye and said:
"Ain't you 'shamed, you sleepy-head!"

Now that you know just about all there is to know about using grass, the big question becomes, "Should I try it?" Of course, it *is* against the law and if you try it you might get caught and go to jail. Very well then. The answer is "No."

However (you didn't think we'd leave it like that, did you?) let's examine the law regarding marijuana in terms of its validity. If it's an invalid law, if it's a harmful law, then it should be changed. If it's a good law, then it should not be changed, and it should be obeyed.

Where do laws come from and what purpose do they serve? In a state of nature there is no organized body of laws. An animal is born free—that is, he can do whatever he wishes—but, of course, the other animals can do whatever they wish, too, and sometimes these wishes conflict. When that happens, only the stronger can act out his wish. The other cannot. As a matter of fact, the other may even be killed. It's the old law of the jungle that we've heard so much about in song and story.

In effect, then, in a state of nature, each animal has total freedom, but absolutely no rights. By "freedom" we mean the absence of antecedent causal determination acting on a decision; by "right" we mean that power, privilege or condition of existence which is granted by others. To try to simplify what are almost indefinable words, "freedoms" are those things you want to do, and "rights" are those things you are allowed to do.

Where do rights come from? They come from contracts, from trading. An individual gives up one freedom to ensure the right to practice another without harm. Animals, of course, don't do this, but people do. People, imbued with intelligence, sophistication, a sense of morality, and an understanding of their inextricable dependency on their fellow man make contracts and effect trades. They trade freedoms for rights.

To illustrate, Dick gets the right to keep Jane out of his house any time he wants by giving up the freedom to go into Jane's house any time he wants. (In other words, you have the *right* to keep people out of your home whenever you want, by giving up the *freedom* to go into other people's homes whenever you want.)

When people choose to live together in a society they agree to give up certain freedoms in order to ensure other freedoms.

Society's legal purpose, then, is to make and enforce laws which ensure the individuals of that society the right granted to them by the other individuals of that society. And in return, the individuals of that society work to keep the society together and functioning.

It follows then that society can only make laws restricting certain freedoms of individuals only to the extent that the exercise of those freedoms might affect other individuals, of the society as a whole. Thus, an individual has the right (given by society) to live with no constraints on his freedom except when those freedoms would act to constrain the freedoms of others.

We're sure that everyone knows this, but we've restated it here because it leads to this, the important point of our discussion: Society, before it abridges the freedom of its members must show that the exercise of that freedom would prove detrimental to the society as a whole, or to the other individual members of it. If society abridges freedoms for other reasons, then it is a totalitarian society. It is a society organized for the benefit of a few—the law makers—and not for the benefit of all.

Now, let's discuss the laws regarding marijuana within this framework. Does the use of marijuana by an individual infringe on the freedom of other individuals? We maintain that it does not. Does the use of marijuana harm the structure of society as a whole? We maintain that it does not. And let's assume that you go one step beyond what we've said earlier, that is, that you believe that society has the right to make laws protecting an individual *from himself*. The question then is, does the use of marijuana harm the individual who uses it? We maintain that it does not.

We, the writers of this book, are now confronted with a problem. We have amassed a tremendous number of quotes, studies and research reports which lead us to the conclusion that marijuana is not harmful in any way to the user, to other members of society or to society as a whole, but we feel that an inclusion of this material is beyond the scope of this book. In the preface we have recommended a number of books which we feel cover this material sufficiently. We hope you'll read the other books.

Assuming that you accept all that we've said here, you then might ask, *"Why is marijuana against the law?"* The foreword and introduction to *The Marihuana Papers* (see preface) give an excellent accounting of the history of the Federal laws. To summarize it briefly, the law was a fraud perpetrated on the American public by a power hungry politician aided by a circulation hungry newspaper publisher. Is that really possible? Of course. If you argue long and loud about something of which people know very little, and if you appeal to their emotions and fears, and if you give them lies and half truths which they have no way of checking, they will believe you. Why shouldn't they? You sound right, they have no information to the contrary, and it doesn't really matter to them anyway. So the lawmakers believed these unscrupulous people, and made unscrupulous laws.

Why has marijuana remained against the law in the face of open protests on the part of thousands of respected members of American society, and in the face of medical and other scientific studies which have failed to find marijuana harmful? Fear! Fear on the part of most Americans which is projected onto their more knowing but politically astute representatives. And it is the fear known as xenophobia: the fear of the unknown. Xenophobia is a survival factor and is part of the genetic code of almost all organisms. If an organism perceives something which is unknown, it moves rapidly away because the unknown often contains dangers. Those animals who ran from the unknown lived to reproduce and transmit this instinctive fear. Those who didn't were often killed, and thus did not transmit this *lack* of fear to offspring. Thus it is normal, and maybe even desirable, to fear the unknown. But progress would never be accomplished if it weren't for those who dare the unknown; who swallow their fear and firmly march ahead.

What about using marijuana is so frightening to all those people who haven't tried it? What are they afraid of? Themselves?

Marijuana changes to some degree one's perception of reality. Everything which occurs when stoned is heightened—and perhaps this is where the fear comes from. But it all resolves into this: if you fear what you might discover about the world or about yourself when stoned, and if this fear overrides your desire for all the new harmless but exciting and meaningful pleasures that marijuana promises, then don't use marijuana. But don't impose your fears of your own inabilities or your own failings on everybody else. Why should our friend Ernie Lundquist have to go to jail for a few years simply because you're afraid that you might discover that you're a homosexual, a failure, ugly, unloved, a communist, a capitalist, a genius, beautiful, or God?

Xenophobia is also the cause of the desire to keep the status quo. The conservative always wants to keep things as they are because he understands things as they are, and is not afraid. The ultra-conservative wants to maintain a state called the status quo ante, which means a return to the past. That is even more knowable and thus safer than the present. Every new thought, every new idea, every new philosophy or discovery has been fought by The Establishment of the day. The Establishment, those in power, is always afraid of losing that power (which is as it should be), and suppresses that which threatens that power—and the unknown is a threat.

Poor old Galileo spent the last eight years of his life in jail because he proved that the earth was not the center of the world. Just think what would have happened to him if he had added that he thought that grass was good.

Now you know the purpose of laws, how we came to have the present marijuana laws, and why these laws have not been changed. Are the marijuana laws good laws? We believe that they are not only *not* good laws, but that they are dangerous laws. They are creating an entirely new criminal class by making felons of people who have done no harm to society, other individuals, or themselves. There are presently something like 25,000 people in prison for violations of the marijuana laws. What happens to these people who now have felony records, who have lost their right to vote, and who have been living closely with hardened anti-social dangerous people? We doubt very much that they will become Scout Masters or cheer leaders.

These laws not only convert law abiding peaceful citizens who were caught with grass into frustrated non-productive hostile criminals, but they polarize society and create a fabric of distrust of friends and disrespect for officials and for *all* laws, good and bad.

Should bad laws be obeyed? Well, they obviously should be changed, but until they are, every man must weigh in his own conscience what he can do to change them, and what he should do about obeying them until they are changed.

People Who Haven't Smoked Grass

Winnie Ruth Judd
Adolf Hitler
Richard Nixon
Thomas Dewey
Muriel Humphrey
Your Mother
Your Father
My Mother
My Father
Lester Maddox
Regis Philbin
Howard Johnson
Ayn Rand
Jack LaLanne
Edgar Guest
Shirley Temple
Ronald and Nancy Reagan
Ulysses S. Grant

Dangerous Plants

One significant aspect of the human mind is its quench-less searching for knowledge. Today man's curiosity reaches out as far as the quasars and deep within the atom. But one of the most exciting scientific adventures is the probing of the human mind, and scientists are not alone in their probing. Today millions of people, and people of every kind, have undertaken the study of the human mind. Some through therapy, some through the meditative processes of Zen and Yoga, and some through the drug experience.

We have found many kinds of chemicals, drugs, narcotics, and mind alterers, to help us in our search. Many of them, although successful to some degree in adding to our store of knowledge, are potentially dangerous, and have been made illegal. The fact that they are illegal may make them more difficult to obtain, but it does not put out the fire of curiosity. And as each one becomes illegal, another one comes to take its place. This, we believe, is good. Man's spirit, along with his curiosity, is not easily killed.

Marijuana is used by millions of people in the United States, in spite of its illegality. These people find that marijuana produces many desirable and harmless effects, and when they are unable to find marijuana, some of them may try to find a replacement. If marijuana, a simple plant, causes such great feelings, they reason, why isn't it possible that other plants will also produce like feelings. And so, armed with this simple logic, they go wandering through fields, glens, dales, and those kinds of places, smoking or eating various plants as their fancy or muse dictates. Some of these may produce a mild high, but many are lethal.

Below you will find a list of plants which can cause severe illness or death, and thus should be avoided.

This information comes from the National Safety Council, inter alia, and is by no means complete. To the axiom, "Know your connection," we could also add, "Know your garden."

Azalea	Mountain laurel
Buttercup	Nightshade
Castor beans	Oleander
Daffodil bulbs	Poinsettia
Hemlock	Poison ivy, oak, and sumac
Hydrangea	Red sage
Jack-in-the pulpit	Rhododendron
Jasmine	Rhubarb leaves
Jimson weed	Wisteria
Lily of the valley	Yew

The Criminal Penalties Under the Current Marijuana Laws

NOTE: The material in this Appendix was provided by the National Organization for the Reform of Marijuana Laws (NORML), and we gratefully acknowledge their help.

We urge you to support NORML. For the complete story of their immense accomplishments, see the interview with Keith Stroup in the February 1977 issue of Playboy Magazine. NORML's offices are located at 2317 M St., N.W., Washington, D.C. 20037. Membership is only $15.00 per year.

NORML's Statement of Purpose

NORML is a non-profit public interest lobby working to remove the criminal penalties for the possession and use of marijuana, a step recommended by the President's Commission on Marijuana and Drug Abuse. NORML does not advocate the use of marijuana. We do believe, however, that the burdensome costs of continued criminal prohibition far exceed any deterrent value of the present laws. Our society can no longer afford to pay the price of ruined lives and careers, wasted economic resources and ineffective drug education programs by trying to pursue and arrest the 35 million people in the United States who have now used marijuana.

Our country's drug laws should be in accord with

the most accurate information available, and based on the possibility of harm presented by a particular drug; not on prejudice, fear, or moral fervor. Thomas Jefferson insisted that, ". . . laws and institutions must go hand in hand with the progress of the human mind." Since we now know that marijuana is a relatively harmless drug, we should change our laws to reflect that fact. NORML supports a policy of discouragement for all recreational drug use, but our society can not continue to make criminals out of those individuals who choose to ignore our advice.

The data appearing in the following tables is current as of September, 1977.

Table I

The Federal Law: The Controlled Substances Act of 1970, Pub. Law 91-513 (Oct. 27, 1970)

OFFENSE	1st Offense	2nd Offense	Subsequent Offense
Simple possession	0-1 year, $5,000 [1]	0-2 years, $10,000	Same
Possession with intent to distribute	0-5 years, $15,000	0-10 years, $30,000	Same
Sale or distribution	0-5 years, $15,000 [2]	0-10 years, $30,000	Same
Sale or distribution to a minor	0-10 years, $30,000	0-15 years, $45,000	Same

[1] For first offender, court has discretionary authority to defer proceedings and place defendant on probation, which, if successfully discharged, avoids an adjudication of guilt. For offenders under 21, court has further discretionary authority to completely expunge the records.

[2] Distribution of a "small amount of marijuana for no remuneration" is to be treated the same as simple possession.

Table II

State Penalties for Possession of Marijuana

(All fines are represented as maximum amounts possible)

State	Amount	First Offense	Second Offense	Subsequent Offense
Alabama	any amount	0-1 yr. and/or $1,000	2-15 yrs. and/or $25,000	same
Alaska	any amount in private for personal use, or up to 1 oz. in public	$100 fine only	same	same
	more than 1 oz. in public	0-1 yr. and/or $1,000	same	same
	any amount while driving a motor vehicle	$1,000 fine only	same	same
Arizona	any amount	0-1 yr. in county jail and/or $1,000; or 1-10 yrs. in state prison and/or $50,000	2-20 yrs. and/or $50,000	5 yrs.-life and/or $50,000
Arkansas	any amount	0-1 yr. and/or $250	0-2 yrs. and/or $500	2-5 yrs.
California	up to 1 oz.	$100 fine only	same	same
	more than 1 oz.	0-6 mos. and/or $500	same	same

123

State	Amount	First Offense	Second Offense	Subsequent Offense
Colorado	up to 1 oz.	$100 fine only	same	same
	more than 1 oz.	0-1 yr. and/or $500	0-2 yrs. and/or $500-$1,000	1-14 yrs. and/or $1,000-$2,000
	public display or consumption of up to 1 oz.	0-15 days and mandatory $100 fine	same	same
Connecticut	up to 4 ozs.	0-1 yr. and/or $1,000	0-5 yrs. and/or $3,000	same
	more than 4.ozs.	015 yrs. and/or $2,000	0-10 yrs. and/or $5,000	same
Delaware	any amount	0-2 yrs. and/or $500	0-7 yrs. and/or $500	same
Florida	up to 5 grams	0-1 yr. and/or $1,000	0-3 yrs. and/or $1,000	same
	more than 5 grams	0-5 yrs. and/or $5,000	0-10 yrs. and/or $5,000	same
Georgia	up to 1 oz.	0-1 yr. and/or $1,000	same	same
	more than 1 oz.	1-10 yrs.	same	same
Hawaii	up to 1 oz.	0-30 days and/or $500	same	same
	1 oz.-2.2 lbs.	0-1 yr. and/or $1,000	same	same
	more than 2.2 lbs.	0-5 yrs. and/or $5,000	same	same
Idaho	up to 3 ozs.	0-1 yr. and/or $1,000	0-2 yrs. and/or $2,000	same
	more than 3 ozs.	0-5 yrs. and/or $15,000	0-10 yrs. and/or $30,000	same

State	Amount	First Offense	Second Offense	Subsequent Offense
Illinois	up to 2.5 grams	0-30 days and/or $500	same	same
	2.5-10 grams	0-6 mos. and/or $500	same	same
	10-30 grams	0-1 yr. and/or $1,000	1-3 yrs. and/or $10,000	same
	30-500 grams	1-3 yrs. and/or $10,000	1-10 yrs. and/or $10,000	same
	more than 500 grams	1-10 yrs. and/or $10,000	1-20 yrs. and/or $10,000	same
Indiana	up to 30 grams	0-1 yr. and/or $5,000	same	same
	more than 30 grams	2-4 yrs. and/or $10,000; or 0-1 yr. and/or $5,000	same	2-14 yrs.
Iowa	any amount	0-6 mos. and/or $1,000	0-18 mos. and/or $3,000	same
Kansas	any amount	0-1 yr. and/or $2,500	0-10 yrs. and/or $5,000	same
Kentucky	any amount	0-90 days and/or $250	same	same
Louisiana	any amount	0-6 mos. and/or $500	0-5 yrs. and/or $2,000	0-20 yrs., w/ or w/o hard labor
Maine	any amount for personal use	$200 fine only	same	same
Maryland	any amount	0-1 yr. and/or $1,000	0-2 yrs. and/or $2,000	same
Massachusetts	any amount	0-6 mos. and/or $500	0-2 yrs. and/or $2,000	same
Michigan	up to 2 ozs.	0-1 yr. and/or $1,000	0-2 yrs. and/or $2,000	same
	more than 2 ozs.	0-4 yrs. and/or $2,000	0-8 yrs. and/or $4,000	same

State	Amount	First Offense	Second Offense	Subsequent Offense
Minnesota	up to 1½ ozs.	$100 fine only	0-90 days and/or $300 [1]	same
	more than 1½ ozs.	0-3 yrs. and/or $3,000	0-6 yrs. and/or $6,000	same
	more than .05 oz. while driving a motor vehicle	0-90 days and/or $300	same	same
Mississippi	up to 1 oz.	$100-$250 fine	$250 fine and 5-60 days	$250-$500 fine and 5-180 days
	if driving	$500 fine and up to 90 days	———	———
Missouri	more than 1 oz.	0-3 yrs. and/or $3,000	0-6 yrs. and/or $6,000	same
	up to 35 grams	0-1 yr. and/or $1,000	0-5 yrs. and/or $1,000	same
	more than 35 grams	0-5 yrs. and/or $1,000	5 yrs.-life	10 yrs.-life
Montana	up to 60 grams	0-1 yr. and/or $1,000	0-3 yrs. and/or $1,000	same
	more than 60 grams	0-5 yrs.	same	same
Nebraska	up to 1 lb.	0-7 days and/or $500	0-14 days and/or $1,000	same
	more than 1 lb.	0-6 mos. in county jail or 1 yr. in state prison and/or $500	0-1 yr. in county jail or 2 yrs. in state prison and/or $1,000	same

[1] A second violation within a two-year period is subject to 0-90 days and/or $300, and participation in a diagnostic examination for chemical dependency.

State	Amount	First Offense	Second Offense	Subsequent Offense
Nevada [2]	any amount by person over age 21	1-6 yrs. and/or $2,000	1-10 yrs. and/or $2,000	1-20 yrs. and/or $5,000
	up to 1 oz. by person under age 21	0-1 yr. and/or $1,000	1-6 yrs. and/or $2,000	1-10 yrs.
New Hampshire	up to 1 lb.	0-1 yr. and/or $1,000	0-7 yrs. and/or $2,000	same
	more than 1 lb.	0-7 yrs. and/or $2,000	0-15 yrs. and/or $2,000	same
New Jersey [2]	up to 25 grams	0-6 mos. and/or $500	same	same
	more than 25 grams	0-5 yrs. and/or $15,000	same	same
New Mexico [2]	up to 1 oz.	0-15 days and/or $50-$100	0-1 yr. and/or $100-$1,000	same
	1-8 ozs.	0-1 yr. and/or $100-$1,000	same	same
	more than 8 ozs.	1-5 yrs. and/or $5,000	same	same
New York [2]	up to 25 grams	$100 fine	$200 fine	0-15 days and/or $250 fine
	over 25 grams or any public use or display	$500 fine or 3 mos.	same	same
	over 2 ozs.	$1000 fine and/or 0-1 yr.	same	same
	over 8 ozs.	0-4 yrs.	same	same
	over 16 ozs.	0-7 yrs.	same	same

127

State	Amount	First Offense	Second Offense	Subsequent Offense
North Carolina [2]	over 10 lbs.	0-15 yrs.	same	same
	up to 1 oz.	$100 fine	$500 fine and/or 0-6 mos.	same
	more than 1 oz.	0-5 yrs. and/or $5,000	5-10 yrs. and/or $10,000	10-30 yrs. and/or $30,000
North Dakota [2]	any amount	0-1 yr. and/or $1,000	0-2 yrs. and/or $2,000	same
Ohio	up to 100 grams	$100 fine only	same	same
	100-200 grams	0-30 days and/or $250	same	same
	200-600 grams	6 mos.-5 yrs. and/or $2,500	1-10 yrs. and/or $5,000	same
	more than 600 grams	1-10 yrs. and/or $5,000	2-15 yrs. and/or $7,500	same
Oklahoma [2]	any amount	0-1 yr.	2-10 yrs.	same
Oregon	up to 1 oz.	$100 fine only	same	same
	more than 1 oz.	0-10 yrs. and/or $2,500	same	same
Pennsylvania [2]	up to 30 grams	0-30 days and/or $500	same	same
	more than 30 grams	0-1 yr. and/or $5,000	same	same
Rhode Island	any amount	0-1 yr. and/or $500	0-2 yrs. and/or $1,000	same
South Carolina [2]	up to 1 oz.	0-3 mos. and/or $100	0-6 mos. and/or $200	same
	more than 1 oz.	0-6 mos. and/or $1,000	0-1 yr. and/or $2,000	same

State	Amount	First Offense	Second Offense	Subsequent Offense
South Dakota	up to 1 oz.	$100 fine and/or up to 30 days in jail	same	same
	1 oz.-1 lb.	0-1 yr. and/or $1,000	same	same
	more than 1 lb.	0-2 yrs. and/or $2,000	same	same
Tennessee	any amount	0-1 yr. and/or $1,000	1-2 yrs.	2-3 yrs.
Texas [2]	up to 2 ozs.	0-6 mos. and/or $1,000	30 days-6 mos. and/or $1,000	same
	2 ozs.-4 ozs.	0-1 yr. and/or $2,000	90 days-1 yr. and/or $2,000	same
	more than 4 ozs.	2-10 yrs. and/or $5,000	2-20 yrs. and/or $10,000	same
Utah [2]	any amount	0-6 mos. and/or $299	0-1 yr. and/or $1,000	0-5 yrs.
Vermont	any amount	0-6 mos. and/or $500	0-2 yrs. and/or $2,000	same
Virginia [2]	any amount	0-1 yr. and/or $1,000	same	same
Washington	up to 40 grams	0-90 days and/or $250	same	same
	more than 40 grams	0-5 yrs. and/or $10,000	0-10 yrs. and/or $10,000	same
West Virginia [2]	any amount	90 days-6 mos. and/or $1,000	same	same
Wisconsin [2]	any amount	0-1 yr. and/or $250	0-2 yrs. and/or $500	same

State	Amount	First Offense	Second Offense	Subsequent Offense
Wyoming [2]	any amount	0-6 mos. and/or $1,000	same	0-5 yrs. and/or $5,000
District of Columbia	any amount	0-1 yr. and/or $100-$1,000	0-10 yrs. and/or $500-$5,000	same

[2] Conditional discharge for first offense possession.

Table III

State Penalties for Possession with Intent to Distribute and Sale of Marijuana

(All fines represented as maximum amounts possible.)

State	Possession with Intent to Distribute		Sale	
	First offense	Second offense	First offense	Second offense
Alabama	2-15 yrs. and/or $25,000	4-30 yrs. and/or $50,000	2-15 yrs. and/or $25,000	4-30 yrs. and/or $50,000
Alaska	0-25 yrs. and/or $20,000	0-life and/or $25,000	0-25 yrs. and/or $20,000	0-life and/or $25,000
Arizona	2-10 yrs. and/or $50,000	5-15 yrs. and/or $50,000	5 yrs.-life and/or $50,000	5 yrs.-life and/or $50,000
Arkansas 1	3-10 yrs. and/or $15,000	3-20 yrs. and/or $30,000	3-10 yrs. and/or $15,000	3-20 yrs. and/or $30,000

There is a rebuttable presumption that possession of more than 1 oz. of marijuana is with an intent to distribute.

	Possession with Intent to Distribute		Sale	
	First offense	Second offense	First offense	Second offense
California (Effective: July 1, 1977)[2]	16 mos., 2 yrs., or 3 yrs.	Same	2, 3, or 4 yrs.	Same
Colorado	1-14 yrs. and/or $1,000	Same	3-14 yrs. and/or $10,000	5-30 yrs. and/or $10,000
Connecticut	0-7 yrs. and/or $1,000	0-15 yrs. and/or $5,000	0-7 yrs. and/or $1,000	0-15 yrs. and/or $5,000
Delaware	0-10 yrs. and $1,000-$10,000	3-15 yrs. and $1,000-$10,000	0-10 yrs. and $1,000-$10,000	3-15 yrs. and $1,000-$10,000
Florida	0-5 yrs. and/or $5,000	0-10 yrs. and/or $5,000	0-5 yrs. and/or $5,000	0-10 yrs. and/or $5,000
Georgia	1-10 yrs.	Same[3]	Same	Same[3]

[2] These penalties are contained in S.B. 42, adopted August, 1976, effective July 1, 1977. The judge will select a fixed term of imprisonment from the three alternatives set out above. The middle sentence must be imposed unless there are aggravating circumstances (the higher penalty will then be imposed) or mitigating circumstances (the lower penalty will then be imposed). Until S.B. 42 takes effect, possession with intent to distribute is subject to 2-10 yrs., up to life for third offense, and sale is subject to 5 yrs.-life.

[3] This statute's general multiple-offender provision provides that if the person was sentenced to a term in prison for the first offense, the maximum penalty must be given for subsequent offenses. It is presently being litigated whether this general provision applies to marijuana offenders.

State	Possession with Intent to Distribute		Sale	
	First offense	Second offense	First offense	Second offense
Hawaii	No such offense		Up to 2 ozs., 0-1 yr. and/or $1,000; more than 2 ozs., 0-5 yrs. and/or $5,000	Same
Idaho	0-5 yrs. and/or $15,000	0-10 yrs. and/or $30,000	0-5 yrs. and/or $15,000	0-10 yrs. and/or $30,000
Illinois	Less than 2.5 gms., 0-6 mos. and/or $500; 2.5-10 gms., 0-1 yr. and/or $1,000; 10-30 gms., 1-3 yrs. and/or $10,000; 30-500 gms., 1-10 yrs. and/or $10,000; More than 500 gms., 1-20 yrs. and/or $10,000	Same	Less than 2.5 gms., 0-6 mos. and/or $500; 2.5-10 gms., 0-1 yr. and/or $1,000; 10-30 gms., 1-3 yrs. and/or $10,000; 30-500 gms., 1-10 yrs. and/or $10,000; More than 500 gms., 1-20 yrs. and/or $10,000	Same

State	Possession with Intent to Distribute		Sale	
	First offense	Second offense	First offense	Second offense
Indiana (Effective: July 1, 1977)[4]	Up to 30 gms., 0-1 yr. and/or $5,000	Same	Same	Same
	More than 30 gms., 2-4 yrs. and/or $10,000; or 0-1 yr. and/or $5,000	Same	Same	Same
Iowa[5]	5 yrs. mandatory and/or $1,000	5-15 yrs. and/or $3,000	5 yrs. mandatory and/or $1,000	5-15 yrs. and/or $3,000
Kansas	0-10 yrs. and/or $5,000	Same	0-10 yrs. and/or $5,000	Same
Kentucky	0-1 yr. and/or $500	1-5 yrs. and/or $3,000-$5,000	0-1 yr. and/or $500	1-5 yrs. and/or $3,000-$5,000

[4] These provisions are contained in P.L. 148, Sec. 7, Acts. of 1976, effective July 1, 1977. Until that date, possession with intent to distribute or sale of up to 30 grams is subject to 0-1 yr. and/or $500 for first offense, 0-2 yrs. and/or $1,000 for second offense. Possession with intent to distribute or sale of more than 30 grams is subject to 1-20 yrs. and/or $2,000 for first offense, 1-40 yrs. and/or $4,000 for second offense.

[5] An essential element of the possession with intent to distribute and sale offenses is that they must be committed with an intent to profit, rather than as an accommodation. If this is not proven, the defendant will be sentenced under the simple possession penalties.

State	Possession with Intent to Distribute		Sale	
	First offense	Second offense	First offense	Second offense
Louisiana	0-10 yrs. and/or $15,000	0-20 yrs. and/or $30,000	0-10 yrs. and/or $15,000	0-20 yrs. and/or $30,000
Maine [6]	0-1 yr. and/or $500	Same	0-1 yr. and/or $500	Same
Maryland	0-5 yrs. and/or $15,000	0-10 yrs. and/or $30,000	0-5 yrs. and/or $15,000	0-10 yrs. and/or $30,000
Massachusetts	0-2 yrs. and/or $5,000	2-5 yrs. and/or $10,000	0-2 yrs. and/or $5,000	2-5 yrs. and/or $10,000
Michigan	0-4 yrs. and/or $2,000	0-8 yrs. and/or $4,000	0-4 yrs. and/or $2,000	0-8 yrs. and/or $4,000
Minnesota	0-5 yrs. and/or $15,000	1-10 yrs. and/or $30,000	0-5 yrs. and/or $15,000	1-10 yrs. and/or $30,000
Mississippi	0-10 yrs. and/or $15,000	0-20 yrs. and/or $30,000	0-20 yrs. and/or $30,000	0-40 yrs. and/or $60,000
Missouri	No such offense	Same	5 yrs.-life	10 yrs.-life
Montana	0-20 yrs.,	Same	1 yr.-life	Same
Nebraska	0-6 mos. in county jail or 1-5 yrs. in prison and/or $2,000	0-12 mos. in county jail or 2-10 yrs. in prison and/or $4,000	0-6 mos. in county jail or 1-5 yrs. in prison and/or $2,000	0-1 yr. in county jail or 2-10 yrs. in prison and/or $4,000

[6] There is a rebuttable presumption that possession of more than 1½ ozs. is with an intent to distribute.

State	Possession with Intent to Distribute		Sale	
	First offense	Second offense	First offense	Second offense
Nevada	No such offense	Same	1-20 yrs. and/or $5,000	0-life and/or $5,000
New Hampshire	No such offense		0-15 yrs. and/or $2,000	Same
New Jersey	0-5 yrs. and/or $15,000	0-10 yrs. and/or $30,000	0-5 yrs. and/or $15,000	0-10 yrs. and/or $30,000
New Mexico	1-5 yrs. and/or $5,000	2-10 yrs. and/or $5,000	1-5 yrs. and/or $5,000	2-10 yrs. and/or $5,000
New York	0-7 yrs.	3-7 yrs. (Must serve ½ of sentence)	1-15 yrs.	6-15 yrs. (Must serve ½ of sentence)
North Carolina	0-5 yrs. and/or $5,000	5-10 yrs. and/or $10,000	0-5 yrs. and/or $5,000	5-10 yrs. and/or $10,000
North Dakota	0-10 yrs. and/or $10,000	0-20 yrs. and/or $20,000	0-10 yrs. and/or $10,000	0-20 yrs. and/or $20,000
Ohio	No such offense	Same	Up to 200 gms., 6 mos.-5 yrs. and/or $2,500; 200-600 gms., 1-10 yrs. and/or $5,000;	Up to 200 gms., 1-10 yrs. and/or $5,000; 200-600 gms., 2-15 yrs. and/or $7,500;

State	Possession with Intent to Distribute		Sale	
	First offense	Second offense	First offense	Second offense
Oklahoma	2-10 yrs. and/or $5,000	4-20 yrs. and/or $10,000	Over 600 gms., 2-15 yrs. (6 mos. mandatory) and/or $7,500	Over 600 gms., 2-15 yrs. (1 yr. mandatory) and/or $7,500
Oregon	0-10 yrs. and/or $2,500	Same	0-10 yrs. and/or $2,500	4-20 yrs. and/or $10,000
Pennsylvania	0-5 yrs. and/or $15,000	0-10 yrs. and/or $30,000	0-5 yrs. and/or $15,000	Same
Rhode Island	0-30 yrs. and/or $50,000	0-60 yrs. and/or $100,000	0-30 yrs. and/or $50,000	0-10 yrs. and/or $30,000
South Carolina	0-5 yrs. and/or $5,000	0-10 yrs. and/or $10,000	0-5 yrs. and/or $5,000	0-60 yrs. and/or $100,000
South Dakota	No such offense	Same	Up to 1 oz, 0-1 yr. and/or $1,000; 1 oz.-1 lb, 0-2 yrs. and/or $2,000; 1 lb. or more, 0-5 yrs. and/or $5,000	0-10 yrs. and/or $10,000

137

State	Possession with Intent to Distribute		Sale	
	First offense	Second offense	First offense	Second offense
Tennessee	Up to ½ oz., 0-1 yr. and/or $1,000; More than ½ oz., 1-5 yrs. and/or $3,000	Up to ½ oz., 1-2 yrs.; More than ½ oz., 1-10 yrs. and/or $6,000	Up to ½ oz., 0-1 yr. and/or $1,000; More than ½ oz., 1-5 yrs. and/or $3,000	Up to ½ oz., 1-2 yrs.; More than ½ oz., 1-10 yrs. and/or $6,000
Texas	No such offense	Same	2-10 yrs. and/or $5,000	2-20 yrs. and/or $10,000
Utah	0-5 yrs. and/or $5,000	Same	0-5 yrs. and/or $5,000	Same
Vermont	more than ½ oz. or 25 cigarettes, 0-2 yrs. and/or $2,000; more than 2 ozs. or 100 cigarettes, 0-5 yrs. and/or $5,000	Same	0-5 yrs. and/or $10,000	10-25 yrs. and/or $25,000
Virginia	5-40 yrs. and/or $25,000	Same	5-40 yrs. and/or $25,000	Same
Washington	0-5 yrs. and/or $10,000	0-10 yrs. and/or $20,000	0-5 yrs. and/or $10,000	0-10 yrs. and/or $20,000

State	Possession with Intent to Distribute		Sale	
	First offense	Second offense	First offense	Second offense
West Virginia	1-5 yrs. and/or $15,000	1-10 yrs. and/or $30,000	1-5 yrs. and/or $15,000	1-10 yrs. and/or $30,000
Wisconsin	0-5 yrs. and/or $15,000	0-10 yrs. and/or $30,000	0-5 yrs. and/or $15,000	0-10 yrs. and/or $30,000
Wyoming	0-10 yrs. and/or $10,000	0-20 yrs. and/or $20,000	0-10 yrs. and/or $10,000	0-20 yrs. and/or $20,000
District of Columbia	No such offense	Same	0-1 yr. and/or $100-1,000	0-10 yrs. and/or $500-5,000

Table IV

Federal Marijuana Penalties

(All fines represented as maximum amounts possible.)

Offense	First Offense	Second Offense	Subsequent Offense
Simple possession	0-1 yr. and/or $5,000 [1]	0-2 yrs. and/or $10,000	Same
Possession with intent to distribute	0-5 yrs. and/or $15,000	0-10 yrs. and/or $30,000	Same
Sale or distribution	0-5 yrs. and/or $15,000 [2]	0-10 yrs. and/or $30,000	Same
Sale or distribution to a minor	0-10 yrs. and/or $30,000	0-15 yrs. and/or $45,000	Same

Note: These penalties are contained in the Federal Controlled Substances Act of 1970, 21 U.S.C. Sec. 801 *et seq.*

[1] For first offenders, the court has discretionary authority to defer proceedings and place the defendant on probation, which if successfully discharged, avoids an adjudication of guilt. For offenders under 21, the court has further discretionary authority to completely expunge the records.

[2] Distribution of a "small amount of marijuana for no remuneration" is treated the same as simple possession.

140

LOCAL MARIJUANA ORDINANCES

In 1971, Ann Arbor, Michigan, became the first city to decriminalize marijuana possession. Since that time, at least fourteen other local governments—villages, cities, and counties—have adopted ordinances that call for only a fine and no jail sentence for the possession of small amounts of marijuana. In four cities, the maximum fine is $5.

The ordinances were passed by City or County Councils and in some cases, by voter referendum. About one-half of the states have some provision in their constitutions giving municipalities the option to adopt lower penalties for offenses of local concern.

The Ann Arbor ordinance was originally passed by the City Council, repealed, and later restored by voter referendum. It provides for a maximum $5 fine for the use, posssession, or sale of any quantity of marijuana. Instead of arresting an offender, the ordinance requires police to give a parking-ticket citation. It also requires that the city's parking violation procedures be used for collecting the fine. Additionally, the ordinance expressly forbids city police officers and prosecutors from referring a marijuana case to the state police for prosecution under the state law.

Much of the push for the Ann Arbor ordinance came from students at the city's University of Michigan campus. Three other university towns have also adopted marijuana ordinances—East Lansing, home of Michigan State; Ypsilanti, home of Eastern Michigan University; and Oxford, Ohio, home of Miami University.

The Ypsilanti ordinance, adopted in 1974, and the Oxford ordinance, adopted in 1975, call for a maximum $5 fine for first and subsequent offenses. The East Lansing ordinance, passed in 1971 and later amended, provides for a $5 fine for the first offense, $10 for the second offense and $100 for a third offense.

Though jail penalties are gone, the fines of some local laws can be stiff. In 1976, two villages in Illinois adopted marijuana ordinances and the maximum fine can range up to $500. In Deerfield, possession of up to 30 grams of marijuana (slightly more than 1 ounce), is subject to this fine as is possession, sale or cultivation of up to 10 grams of marijuana in Palantine. Seattle, Washington, also has a $500 maximum fine for possession of marijuana which it adopted in 1974.

In other areas, Atlanta, Georgia, adopted an ordinance in 1976 containing a maximum $250 fine for possession of up to one ounce of marijuana. Six municipalities in Wisconsin also have marijuana ordinances, including Brookfield, Cudahy, Shorewood, South Milwaukee, St. Francis, and West Allis. Their maximum fines range generally from $200 to $250. In Milwaukee County, the Board of Supervisors adopted an ordinance in 1975 making possession of up to an ounce of marijuana on county property subject to a fine of $50-$200, or informal probation.

In many states, local prosecutors and police departments have instituted policies which can operate informally without an ordinance. The policies generally call for citations instead of arrest, or diversion programs instead of prosecution, for minor marijuana cases. For example, the police chief of Austin, Texas, has established a "field release citation program" for persons possessing up to four ounces of marijuana. Dozens of other cities and counties, including Washington, D.C., Sacramento, California, and Cook County, Illinois, have procedures for diverting persons arrested on marijuana charges out of the criminal justice system and into a drug education program.

OTHER MARIJUANA PENALTIES

Cultivation

The penalties for cultivating marijuana are still very harsh in most states. In 30 states, the penalty for cultivation of even one marijuana plant is the same as the penalty for sale of any amount of marijuana. The other 20 states treat cultivation as follows:

In California and Mississippi, the penalty is the same as the penalty for possession with intent to distribute. In Alaska and Maine, cultivation can be treated as either simple possession or possession with intent to distribute. In eight states cultivation has the same penalty as simple possession: Arizona, Indiana, Kansas, Nevada, New York, South Dakota, Texas, Wyoming.

In the other eight states, the penalties are as follows:

> Hawaii—0-5 yrs. and/or $5,000
> Illinois—0-1 yr. and /or $1,000
> Michigan—0-5 yrs. and /or $5,000
> Missouri—6 mos.-1 yr., or 0-20 yrs.
> New Mexico—10-50 yrs. and/or $10,000
> Ohio—6 mos.-5 yrs. and/or $2,500
> Rhode Island—0-20 yrs.
> Tennessee—1-5 yrs. and/or $3,000

In one state—Alaska—cultivation of a small amount of marijuana in private is probably no longer a crime. In 1975, the Supreme Court of Alaska held that adults had a constitutionally-protected right to possess marijuana for personal use in the privacy of the home. *Ravin* v. *State,* 537 P.2d 494 (1975). Cultivation of a small amount of marijuana in the home for personal use appears to be covered by this decision.

Hashish or "Concentrated Cannabis"

Most states do not distinguish between marijuana and concentrated forms of the plant (hashish and hash oil) for penalty purposes. In 31 states and the District of Columbia, possession of concentrated cannabis is subject to the same penalty as possession of marijuana. The other 19 states treat concentrated cannabis as follows:

In seven states, the penalty for possession of any amount of concentrated cannabis is the same as the penalty for possession of more than a specified amount of marijuana:

> Colorado—more than 1 oz.
> Florida—more than 5 gms.
> Minnesota—more than 1½ ozs.
> Mississippi—more than 1 oz.
> Oregon—more than 1 oz.
> South Dakota—more than 1 lb.
> Texas—more than 4 ozs.

In eight states, the penalties for possession of marijuana (M) and concentrated cannabis (CC) are the same, but based upon ratios of the weights of the substances:

Indiana—30 gms. M or 2 gms. CC
Missouri—35 gms. M or 5 gms. CC
Montana—60 gms. M or 1 gm. CC
New Jersey—25 gms. M or 5 gms. CC
North Carolina—1 oz. M or 1/10 oz. CC
Ohio—100 gms. M or 5 gms. hashish or 1 gm. hash oil
Pennsylvania—30 gms. M or 8 gms. CC
South Carolina—1 oz. M or 10 gms. CC

Four other states have separate penalties for possession of concentrated cannabis:

California—0-5 yrs. and/or $5,000 (0-3 yrs. after
   July 1, 1977)
Hawaii—up to ⅛ oz., 0-1 yr. and/or $1,000; ⅛ oz.-
   1 oz., 0-5 yrs. and/or $5,000; more than 1 oz.,
   0-10 yrs. and/or $10,000
Maine—0-1 yr. and/or $500
New Mexico—30 days-1 yr. and/or $500-$1,000

Non-Profit Transfers

Most states still do not distinguish, for penalty purposes, between commercial sales of marijuana and
distribution of small amounts of marijuana between
acquaintances by gift or on a non-profit basis.

In four of the eight states which have decriminalized
possession of marijuana, distribution of marijuana by
gift, or for no remuneration, is treated the same as
simple possession: California (up to 1 oz.), Colorado
(up to 1 oz.), Ohio (up to 20 gms.), and Minnesota
(up to 1½ ozs.).

About 20 other states have lesser penalties for dis-
tributing a small amount of marijuana, non-profit or
by gift, as compared with the penalties for commercial
sale.

Sale to a Minor

Fifteen states and the District of Columbia do not
distinguish, for penalty purposes, between sales of
marijuana to minors or adults: Connecticut, Georgia,
Kansas, Kentucky, Maryland, Massachusetts, Missouri,
Montana, Nebraska, New Hampshire, New York, North
Dakota, South Dakota, Texas, and Vermont.

In eighteen states, the penalty for first offense sale
to a minor is greater than the penalty for first offense
sale to an adult, but less than the penalty for second
offense sale to an adult: Alabama, Arizona, Colorado,
Delaware, Hawaii, Idaho, Iowa, Michigan, Minnesota,

Mississippi, New Jersey, North Carolina, Ohio, Oklahoma, Rhode Island, Washington, Wisconsin, and Wyoming.

In six states, the penalty for first offense sale to a minor is the same as the penalty for second offense sale to an adult: Alaska, Arkansas, Louisiana, New Mexico, Pennsylvania, and South Carolina.

In eleven states, the penalty for first offense sale to a minor is harsher than the penalty for second offense sale to an adult: California, Florida, Illinois, Indiana, Maine, Nevada, Oregon, Tennessee, Utah, Virginia, and West Virginia.

Paraphernalia

Less than a dozen states have laws making it a crime to possess marijuana smoking paraphernalia, and the California legislature abolished this offense in 1975. Some of the laws specifically prohibit "water pipes," "roach clips," and "bongs," but most were drafted in more general language.

Indiana prosecutors have been enjoined from enforcing the state's paraphernalia law. *Indiana NORML* v. *Sendak,* No. TH-75-142-C (S.D. Ind. 1975).

See generally, First Report of the National Commission on Marijuana and Drug Abuse, App., Vol. I, pp. 572-73.

CONSTITUTIONALITY OF MARIJUANA PENALTIES

Courts have declared marijuana penalties unconstitutional on a number of different grounds, including violations of the Right of Privacy, Equal Protection, and Cruel and Unusual Punishment. The most important case was decided by the Supreme Court of Alaska in 1975. The Court held that adults have a constitutionally-protected right to possess or use marijuana in the privacy of the home. *Ravin* v. *State*, 537 P. 2d 494 (1975).

Three other state supreme courts—Washington, Illinois, and Michigan—have held marijuana penalties unconstitutional, as a denial of equal protection, because marijuana was classified with far more dangerous drugs, including narcotics. *State* v. *Zornes*, 469 P. 2d 552 (Wash. 1970); *People* v. *McCabe*, 275 N.E. 2d 407 (Ill. 1971); *People* v. *Sinclair*, 194 N.W. 2d 878 (Mich. 1972).

Courts have also declared penalties for possession and sale of marijuana unconstitutional because they were so excessive that they constituted cruel and unusual punishment. See, *e.g.*, *People* v. *Lorentzen*, 194 N.W. 2d 827 (Mich. 1972); *In re Grant*, 19 Cr. L. Rep. 2545 (Cal. 1976); *People* v. *Ruiz*, 49 C.A. 3d 730 (Cal. 1975); *Downey* v. *Perini*, 518 F. 2d 306 (6th Cir. 1975), vacated and remanded, 44 U.S.L.W. 3330 (1975).

The Supreme Court of New Jersey has held that persons convicted for simple possession of marijuana, first offense, cannot be sentenced to prison unless there are exceptional circumstances. *State* v. *Ward* 270 A. 2d 1 (N.J. 1970).

Other courts have rejected constitutional challenges to marijuana penalties. See generally, Soler, "Of Cannabis and the Courts: A Critical Examination of Constitutional Challenges to Statutory Marijuana Prohibitions," 6 Conn. L. Rev. 601 (1974).

US TREATY OBLIGATIONS

The United States is a party to an international treaty which requires certain controls over marijuana and other substances, the Single Convention on Narcotic Drugs, 18 U.S.T. 1407 (1967). The Single Convention was adopted at a United Nations Conference in New York City in 1961, and more than 100 countries are now parties to it. The U.S. became a party in 1967.

The Single Convention has a carefully and narrowly-drafted definition of marijuana ("cannabis"), which excludes the leaves and seeds (when separated from the flowering tops), and also excludes synthetically produced THC (Tetrahydrocannabinols). For these substances which are not defined as "cannabis," the Single Convention does not require any penalty or sanction whatsoever.

Even for the parts of the marijuana plant which are defined as "cannabis" in the Single Convention—this would include most marijuana consumed in the U.S.—Article 36 of the Single Convention allows each country to, in effect, decide for itself the appropriate penalties to apply. While there can be some debate on the interpretation of Article 36, the following points are supported by the weight of authority, including the sources listed below:

—A party to the Single Convention can, but is not required to, treat the unauthorized possession of marijuana for personal use as a "punishable offense."

—Even if a country considered simple possession a "punishable offense," it would only be required to have imprisonment (jail) penalties for the offense if the country considered it a "serious" offense. If simple possession was not considered a "serious" offense, a lesser sanction would be appropriate, such as a small fine or participation in a drug education program.

—The unauthorized possession of marijuana for commercial distribution, and the unauthorized sale of marijuana, must be treated as "punishable offenses," but again, unless the country believes these offenses are "serious," it can apply such penalties as a small fine or participation in a drug education program.

—The penalty provisions contained in Article 36 are subject to each country's "constitutional limitations," which means that courts in each country can declare marijuana penalties unconstitutional without violating any treaty obligations.

See the official U.N. *Commentary on the Single Convention on Narcotic Drugs, 1961,* prepared by the Secretary-General of the United Nations (1973), at pp. 425-41. See also, Lande, "The International Drug Control System," in Second Report of the National Commission on Marijuana and Drug Abuse, Appendix, Vol. III, pp. 6-132 (March, 1973); Testimony of Donald E. Miller, DEA Chief Counsel, and Lawrence Hoover, former State Department legal advisor, in *NORML* v. *DEA,* hearing held January 28-30, 1975, Transcript pp. 131, 522-25.

MESSAGE FROM THE PRESIDENT OF THE UNITED STATES

The growing drive to decriminalize marijuana recently reached the top levels of government with President Jimmy Carter, taking the first step toward implementing his campaign promise, formally asking Congress to eliminate all federal criminal penalties for possession of one ounce of marijuana. The following is a complete reprint of that section of the August 2nd Presidential message dealing with marijuana policy:

THE WHITE HOUSE
TO THE CONGRESS OF THE UNITED STATES:

Marihuana

Marihuana continues to be an emotional and controversial issue. After four decades, efforts to discourage its use with stringent laws have still not been successful. More than 45 million Americans have tried marihuana and an estimated 11 million are regular users.

Penalties against possession of a drug should not be more damaging to an individual than the use of the drug itself; and where they are, they should be changed. Nowhere is this more clear than in the laws against possession of marihuana in private for personal use. We can, and should, continue to discourage the use of marihuana, but this can be done without defining the smoker as a criminal. States which have already removed criminal penalties for marihuana use, like Oregon and California, have not noted any significant increase in marihuana smoking. The National Commission on Marihuana and Drug Abuse concluded five years ago that marihuana use should be decriminalized, and I believe it is time to implement those basic recommendations.

Therefore, I support legislation amending Federal law to eliminate Federal criminal penalties for the possession of up to one ounce of marihuana. The decriminalization is not legalization. It means only that the Federal penalty for possession would be reduced and a person would receive a fine rather than a criminal penalty. Federal penalties for trafficking would remain in force and the states would remain free to adopt whatever laws they wish concerning the marihuana smoker.

I am especially concerned about the increasing levels of marihuana use, which may be particularly destructive to our youth. While there is certain evidence to date showing that the medical damage from marihuana use may be limited, we should be concerned that chronic intoxication with marihuana or any other drug may deplete productivity, causing people to lose interest in their social environment, their future, and other more constructive ways of filling their free time. In addition, driving while under the influence of marihuana can be very hazardous. I am, therefore, directing the Department of Transportation to expedite its study of the effects of marihuana use on the coordination and reflexes needed for safe driving.

JIMMY CARTER

THE WHITE HOUSE
August 2, 1977

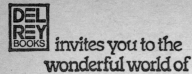